Claire

CAN I LET YOU GO, MY LOVE?

The emotional and spiritual journey of a woman following the loss of her husband.

Kay Van Dijk

Acorn Editions
Cambridge

Acorn Editions
P.O. Box 60
Cambridge
CB1 2NT

British Library Cataloguing in Publication Data:
A catalogue record is available from the British Library.

First published 1997
Reprinted 2003

ISBN 0 9065 5415 2

Printed and bound in Great Britain by
Athenaeum Press Ltd, Gateshead, Tyne & Wear.

To my husband, Job,
and to all those who are left behind to weep.

Acknowledgements

I would like to thank
>   Leonard Suransky
>   Edye Kasteel
>   Willem Glaudemans

for their help and encouragement while reviewing the manuscript and Richard Stienstra for his advice after the completion of this book.

I would also like to thank all those who have supported me during this difficult period of my life.

A very special thanks to my two children, Joy and Björn, for their love and understanding.

Contents

Introduction

I was 47 years old when my husband, Job, died. We had known and loved each other for nearly 20 years.

The poems which follow were mostly written on the spur of the moment as a way of coping with my grief. They would spill out of me in moments of extreme emotion and provide me with some relief.

They should be read as if they were entries in a diary. The fact that they are written in the form of poems should not mislead the reader into thinking that he or she is about to read a volume of poetry. It was essential to me to be able to express my outpourings of grief in simple prose and short phrases, enabling me to release my pent-up feelings without my mind intervening and interrupting this process.

After some time the idea started to grow that maybe others who had lost a loved one could find solace and recognition on reading these 'poems'. If it could relieve some of their isolation and give comfort, then perhaps there would be added meaning to Job's death. For others, this journal may be of help to understand what a grieving relative or friend is going through. The process usually takes far longer than is generally presumed. For outsiders it is difficult to understand the extent to which one's world is devastated by the loss of a loved one.

On reading through this journal, four years after his death, I am struck by the continuous cycle of denial, grief, depression and then partial acceptance only to be followed once more by denial. It is like the peeling of an onion. Each new layer brings one closer to the core; the realisation that the loved one is really and truly dead. Each layer peeled away presents a new shock. The reality of the loss, of that '*never, ever again*' , threatens to come closer, causing once more a rejection of the emotional reality of the death.

In order to follow this process, each poem is dated, in time passed since the death.

Although my mind registered his death, when it happened, it took nine months for me to emotionally begin to accept that he was dead and it was three years and nine months later that I could finally accept that Job, the husband I had loved so much, was really dead. Only then could I emotionally let him go.

This journal is in English and not in Dutch. Although I have lived in Holland for twenty-one years and I speak fluent Dutch, when it comes to expressing myself emotionally I revert back to my mother tongue, English.

For those who have not lost a close loved one, the poems may seem repetitious. Yet it is this seemingly endless cycle of disbelief, pain, grief and depression that so characterises the state of bereavement for me. For those who have lost a loved one, maybe you will find some solace in realising that you are not alone, and that the endless grief, depression or other emotions you are experiencing, are normal, and that given time, yes, it does slowly get better. The wounds do eventually heal.

I also regard this journal as a last tribute to the strong tie that bound Job and myself. A love story that continued through death.

For the English meaning of the Dutch words used in some of the poems, see pages 249-250.

Journal of Poems

Before

Job is dying.
My Job is dying.
Deep, deep inside me
    I know.
Deep, deep inside him
    he knows.
But it stays there
    deep inside.

We cling to straws.
We go through the motions
    of normal life.
He gets thinner and thinner
    and still we think:
'Tomorrow he will get better.
    He conquered it once.
    He will again.'

His strength ebbs.
Like a lion in a cage
    trapped by the walls
        of his impending death.
He paces up and down.
    Up and down
    in rage
        at his narrowing prison.
Rearing to get out.
Growing weaker and weaker.
His efforts becoming
    more and more futile.
Refusing to accept
    the inevitable.

Ten days before he dies,
   he suddenly stops struggling.
Peace descends upon him.
As if he knows
   and accepts
      all that is to come.

Those last days with Job.
However to describe them?
Such intense sorrow.
The precious last moments
   before an impending departure.
Total unreality.
Yet an undercurrent
   urging, forcing,
   him, us
      to feel each moment
      so laden with conflicting emotions.

Scenes spring out
   scorched on the mind forever.
Sitting around his bed.
   All of us crying
      as one.
   A cloud of warmth, love,
      hope, desperation
   Breaking us open
      till we ache in unison.
   The poignant finality
      searing through us.

Emotions too deep for words
　　swirl around the house.
In a daze we hug and comfort
　　one another.
Joined in love and sorrow
　　as the inevitable draws
　　　　inexorably nearer.

One by one
　　he calls the children.
The last confrontation.
The last coming together
　　with Papa.
　　　　For protection.
　　　　For love.
　　　　For measuring one's strength.
Whispered words of wisdom
　　to last a lifetime
　　　　without Papa.

Yes, he says good-bye to the children,
　　his sisters, his friends
　　　　but **not to me**.
The anguish between us is too deep.
It is unthinkable.
A separation – forever
　　just cannot be.
A short journey perhaps
　　and then he will return.
A final good-bye – an absurdity
　　unthinkable.

I move as in a dream.
Calm and strong,
   organising all.
Trying to ease
   the pain and sorrow
      around me.
Protecting Job and myself
   from the reality of being torn apart.
Ignoring the anguished screams
   tearing apart my insides:

"Don't go
   Please don't go.
   Don't leave me.
   I can't live without you."

But these frantic cries
   are buried so deep,
      surrounded by a feeling
         of total unreality.
My big strong Job
   cannot possibly be dying.

✭

16

The Death

Our last night together.
Did I realise it would be
   our last night?

Like a baby you were
   that last day,
      sucking your 'ijsklontjes'.
   So sweetly docile and grateful,
      while I ministered to your needs.
One of the very few times
   that I could take care of you.
You, who were always so strong,
   so self-contained.

In your half dream-like state,
you repeated over and over:
   "Nu wil ik stoppen.
   Nu is het klaar
      met Job.
   Klaar, punt, stop.
   Nu wil ik gaan in het Zelf.
   Zo snel mogelijk naar Huis.
      Het is fantastisch.
      Het is er.
      Nog niet helemaal.
      Het komt...."

Did I realise
   as I lay next to you that evening,
that soon, soon
   you would be gone?

I wanted to go on and on
    looking after you.
For days and days.
    To feel you still.
To touch you forever.

But slowly I realise
    your bright hope during the day,
        of reaching Home,
    has turned into a desperate struggle.
You toss and turn
    in your anguish.
Death eludes you
    again and again.

Slowly it sinks in.
You need help.
I cry out to my guides:
        "Do something.
        Help him to die."
I imagine that I see your silver cord.
Feeling your agony,
    feeling your longing to be gone,
I cut it.

Realising what I have done,
    I break down
    and utter
    the most inhuman howls
    of grief.
Suddenly, like a miracle
    from that world into which you had sunk,
your hand reaches out
    to touch mine
        in comfort,
        in love.

Peace descends upon us.
Our last minutes together.

Then you lift yourself up
    in a superhuman effort.
With far-seeing wild eyes
    you stare into space
    and you cry out in triumph:
        "Je gaat Job!"
My breath stops
    for moments in awe.
Yours forever.

All is now calm.
    Peaceful.
I tidy your limbs, your face, your hair.
    I love you so.
I lie down beside you again,
    very, very close,
    touching you.
So grateful that we are alone.
    Just you and I.

Then I hear you.
I feel
    your words vibrating through me:
        "Het is zo mooi, Kay.
        Niet te beschrijven.
        Fantastisch, heerlijk.
        Wijd, vrij.
        Eindelijk vrij."

My being expands,
   is filled
      with an incredible lightness.
      An immense sense of freedom.
      Indescribable.
Oh, my Job, my Job,
Is this what you are feeling now?
Are you finally happy,
   finally free?

For another hour I cherish
   this glorious, peaceful
      oneness with you.
Until it gradually fades.
And still close,
   oh, so very close,
   still touching you,
I drift in and out of sleep
   for the next few hours,
   till dawn comes,
      and I must break loose from
      these last enchanted moments
      of still being
         so, so close to you
   and announce to the world:
"J. W. van Dijk is dead."

However, months
   and months and months
      will pass
   before I will accept that
'My Job' is no longer alive.

See note 1.

2 days later

Unreality.
Unreal.
He is no longer
   lying beside me,
      but a few feet away
  in his coffin.

I can still touch him
   whenever I want.
And I do, I do.
I run my fingers
   through his thick hair.
Oh, it feels so good, so good,
   my Job.

Who says you are dead?
I can still touch you,
   still feel you.
Now I touch your chest.
It still feels the same,
   a bit cold.... Yes,
      but it is still You.

I promised I would stay with you
   every night.
It is also so comforting
   for me to fall asleep
   sensing you still
   so close by.

See note 2.

The Memorial Service – Three days later

(Written 1½ years later)

I have been so peaceful lately.
Seeming to accept
   your death.

For the first time I dare
   to listen once again
   to the requiem of Fauré
      that was played over and over
      at your funeral service.

It all comes back:
   that evening one and a half years ago.
I am in a state of shock.

Moving in a dream
   of pure unreality.
Screaming inside
   No, No, No.
He is not dead,
He cannot be.

Sustained on the surface
   by your beautiful death,
   by the very nearness of you
      lying close by
         in your coffin.
      And at the same time
         floating
         in the air
         around me.

The children
   bereft,
   uncomprehending.
Held together
   by a tight bond
   of invisible love
     that pours out
     from your centre.

All these people
   gathering to pay you
     their last homage.
Uncomprehending
   of the true state
   of your intrinsic being.

Where are you now
   my Job?
My beautiful Job.
Are you truly
   hovering above us,
     as I so strongly feel,
   living with us,
   feeling our separate emotions?

Oh, my sweet Job.
   I feel you
     so, so close
       and yet so unreachable.

I speak to you
   from the depths of my heart
     before all these people.
Are you proud of me?
I want you to be.

I am doing it for you.
   To pay homage
      to our life together
      to our love
      to the beautiful experience
         that your death was.

I move about
   as if in a dream.
Absorbing the condolences
   as if you were
   beside me.
Knowing how you would have enjoyed
   being here,
   receiving all your dear friends.

The music.
Your chosen music
   plays on
while I move in this
   dream of unreality.

Yes, listening now
   more than a year later
   to that same music.
The wrenching sobs
   now surface
   and explode.
I cry and cry
   wildly
   desperately.
Knowing now
   what it means
   to have lost you.

☆

Memorial Service – 2

So, so personal.
So many people
   sharing
   these very intimate moments
     with me,
     with you,
     with us.

Do they realise?
Can they grasp?
   Your dying.
     So beautiful.
     So agonising.
   Your leaving us
     for another realm.
       Half here,
       half there.
  The momentousness
     of the transition.
Do they realise
   what is happening?

Death.
Torn from one world.
Lanced into another,
   with glory,
   with power,
   with love,
     so much love.

The air
  is emotionally charged.
    Sorrow.
    Disbelief.
    Love.
Each one
  has some bond
    with you.
We are united
  through you.
Each with his own memories.
Each feels
  the tug at his heart.

I open up to everyone.
They are all here for you,
    my love.
    For you.
The last time
  I share you
    with so many.

I feel so so close to you.
So bound up with you.
So exposed
  in my intimate feelings
    for you.

And yet I feel a bond,
  an overflowing
    to all who have come
      to share
        this farewell
          of my beloved.

✯

Memorial Service – 3

Hundreds of people.
Do they realise?
Can they grasp
   what I am losing?
What does it mean
   to them?

Job dead.
Does it sink in?

Can it sink in
   to any of us?
One minute
   so part of this world,
   so active,
   so flesh and blood.
The next
   gone.
Out of sight
   forever.

So much remains.
Yet nothing
   tangible remains.

Death
   the ultimate
   elusive
   mystery.

The Burial

Today we are going to bury you
    my Job.
I don't really believe it.
But I go through the motions.

That big black car in front of us.
How could it possibly be You inside there?

The endless walk at the cemetery.
This enormous hole they have dug.
Now they are lowering your coffin
    that so comfortingly rested in our bedroom
        these past days.

No, No, No.
They cannot.
They cannot
    put you in there.
    In that dark hole
      all alone
      without me.

I can't bear it.
I am going to jump in with you.
I will stay with you always.
I won't leave you alone.
No-one will part us.
Not after all we have been through.
Not after all we have meant to each other.

Now I understand the Indian custom
    of wives being burnt together
        with their beloved one.

Why don't I jump?
I sense the presence
    of those around me.
Reality hits me.
I will crash into the coffin.
I will break my leg.
    I will not die.
    I will not die.
They will not bury me with you.

Oh, Job, oh, Job,
    I can't bear it.
Say it's not happening.
Say it's not true.
Let me wake up.
Wake up and realise,
    this is all a terrible nightmare.

✭

10 days later

The house is quiet now.
Everyone has gone.
Just you and I
   remain.

Imagine everyone thinks
   you are dead.
But of course you can't be.

All those warm letters
   still flowing in every day.
More and more
   'In memoriams'.
More people thinking
   you are dead.

In vain I search the house
   for you.
You must be somewhere.
In the bathroom, I cry:
   "Job, nu is het genoeg.
   Please come back.
   We have had this wonderful experience
      of your death together.
   Now it is over.
   So, please come back.
      Now."

I can't bear it any more.
   Not to be able to touch you.
   To feel your arms around me.
   To feel your love and care
      enveloping me like a soft cushion.

Where are you?
Please, please.
It is enough.
Come back to me.

☆

3 weeks later

Standing in the kitchen
Washing the dishes.
I feel you behind me.
Together we tidy up,
    companionably, harmoniously.
Enjoying a job efficiently done.

Every now and then
    your body brushes against mine.
I feel the warmth spreading.
I smile.
We tease each other.
We laugh.
Love like a soft cloud
    around us.
A sense of belonging, caring.

Yes, yes, I can feel it still
    so vividly.
It can't be gone.
It just can't be.
If I feel it still
    it *must* be there.

That warm soft cloud of love
    settling around my shoulders,
        just behind me
            as you used to be.
So warm, so loving,
    so protective.

You cannot, cannot
    be gone forever.

The grave – 1 month later

All these beautiful flowers,
    blinding in colour,
    so alive.
Tokens of love
    for you.
So many people
    loved you.
Their last tribute.

Every day I rush to you.
The flowers are still alive.
A miracle.
For weeks they live on.
Are you breathing life into them?

It is so peaceful here
    beside you.
I don't really believe
    you are under this earth.
The body I loved so much,
    decaying.
Earth to earth.
Dust to dust.
I would go mad
    if I believed it.

I just don't think.
I feel the peace.
I feel your soft presence.

By tending your grave
   it is as if I am still
   caring for you.
I am drawn here
   again and again.

I have given up
   trying to fathom myself.
I come.
I go.
I just am.

1–7 months later

I walk through the house
   looking for you.
You must be somewhere.

Behind your desk
   where so often you used to sit
   I come to a halt.
I remember how I used to
   stand just here, behind you.
How I ran my fingers
   through your hair
   and down your neck,
     softly, gently,
       so as not to interrupt your work.
Then I moved on,
   somehow sustained, buoyed,
     by the momentary feel of you.

Your chair is empty
   as I stand behind it now.
The loss is so overwhelming
   it threatens to completely
     engulf me.
I can't stand it.
No, no, of course it is not true.

If I search the house,
    if I just look long enough,
    you will be there
        smiling up at me
            from your newspaper,
            from your books.
I will be able
    to feast my eyes
        on you
        once more.

☆

1½ months later

I lie on my bed
   resting.
Tired, empty,
   forlorn, alone,
      longing for you.

If I call him
   surely he will come.
Just as he used to.

You would appear in the doorway.
My heart lifts
   and shifts
      into life, energy.
Just to see you
   walk towards me
      so vital, so alive.

"What is it
   my Kaytje?"
You sit beside me
   just for a moment.
But it is enough,
   enough to feel alive once more.
A quick embrace.
Your body close to mine
   and my motor starts up again.

As you move
   towards the door once more,
      my eyes linger and savour
      your parting body,
   with love, with wonder.

If I call him now
    surely he must come.
I call softly.
I call loudly.
His name echoes wildly
    through the empty house.
Despair, grief.
What if he never comes again?
    I shall die.
    Surely I will.

☆

2 months later

An open wound.

Once a whole.
Complete.

Then wrenched away.
A limb,
   so vital, so dear.

Leaving a gaping, bleeding wound.

Slowly clotting.
Only to be torn apart
   again and again
     as each memory
       pierces through.

Oh, the pain,
   the pain of it.

1–2 months later

I want to sink away,
   lower and lower,
   stiller and stiller,
     die.

Lie on that bed.
Never get up again
   until it is all over.
     Life.

A voice whispers:
   Kay, you must try.
     Please.
   Give yourself a chance
    to find out
      if Life
    is really not worth living
     without *him*.

Give yourself time.
   Three years.

Force yourself
   to get up
   out of that bed.
Move.
Go out.
Feel people.
Anything.
Do anything.
Don't let yourself sink away
   into nothingness.
Not now.
Not yet.

In three years
    I promise you
        if you still feel so lifeless
    you will be able to say:

"I tried,
I truly did everything I could
    but life is not worth living
        without him."

Then I will lie down
    on this bed.
I will give up my will to live
    and finally sink away.

But
    not now.
Not yet,
    Kay.

People – 3 months

They bring me food.
They listen patiently.
They are so kind.
    But they can't take away the pain.

"You can always come."
"Phone when you like."
"We are there for you."
    But they can't take away the emptiness.

I am overwhelmed
    by their warmth,
    by their interest,
    by their love.
        But they can't take away the loss.

No-one is **Him**.
No-one can feel what I feel.
No-one can really help.
In that aching place inside
    I am all alone.

☆

3 months later
(and often thereafter)

Seeing his car.
Strong and reliable.
Big and beautiful.
A sign that says:
   Job is here.
A thrill of joy,
   of contentedness passes through me.

Only now, only now,
   I don't seem to be able to see him any more.
His car is there, so he *must* be there.
Only where, oh where is he?

I sit inside.
His feel is all around me,
   so comforting,
   so close,
   so familiar.
If I close my eyes
   he will appear.
   He must.

Hope changes to grief,
   to despair,
   to apathy.
To grief, grief, grief once more.

✸

5 months later

At home, the illusion of him
   is still all around me.
Here among all these people
   I feel so exposed.

Where are you now
   my Job?
Please, I can't bear to feel
   so unprotected.
Without you at my side
   I feel as if a piece
     of Me
       is missing.

Open and exposed
   for all to see.
I look for a place to hide,
   to run to.
Till once more
   you are there at my side
     for all to see.

No-one can touch me now.
I feel so safe, so safe.
You form an invisible
   beautiful barrier
     between me
     and all those others
     there outside.
Your love
   shelters me,
   cradles me.

Oh, it feels so good, so good.
Your big body
    between me and the world.

You can't *not* be there any more.
I feel so frail.
    I smile, I nod,
        but inside
            is chaos,
            is pain.

Can't they see he is still there,
    somewhere?
Why does everyone think he is dead?
    Really dead.
That he won't come back any more
    or worse still:
They have forgotten you
    or don't know you ever existed.
No, No, No.
In a minute you will surprise them all.
I will feel your arm around my shoulder.
I will hear you say:
    "En dit is mijn Kay."

                  ✮

5 months later

Work finished.
Flowing with satisfaction.
Everything went so well.
Eager to tell all.
I search for you.

The kitchen is dark.
Your chair is empty.
The words die on my lips.
The senselessness of it all
    overwhelms me.

Why do anything any more?
You are no longer there to listen.
    My mirror.
    My other half.
    My keyboard.

The realisation:
So much of what I did,
    I did for You.
Who am I?
What is left
    of what I thought was me?

5 months

Walking with the dog
   to the mailbox.
The path is the same.
The trees are the same.
The same moon and stars.
Yet everything has changed.

I am walking in a different world.
Sorrow, emptiness
   is heavy in the air.

The dog runs, jumps, pulls,
   just like she always used to.
Disbelief.
Make-believe.
He will be there when I reach home.
He can't not be home.
Heaviness as I get closer.
Hope and at the same time
   despair.
Something in me knows.

I hang back.
The darkness comforts.
The silent trees sympathise.

The house looms ahead.
My feet walk.
The dog pulls.
Emptiness waits.

5 months

Driving along the road
   I see a bus
      through the windscreen.
As it passes, the car shudders.
It came very close.

In a split second
   it is as if I see
      the head-on crash.
I feel the flash of joy
   as I leave my body behind
      in the entwined wreckage.
The enormous sense of relief.
It is over, over.
The terrible struggle
   to survive.

Another second passes.
Shock.
Disbelief.
Do I really want to die?
   To let go?

Not yet.
I promised I would give myself
   three years
      to see if life
         was worth living
            without You.

★

6 months

Every night as I close my eyes
    I think:
        tonight, tonight I will see him again,
        hold him again,
            in my dreams.

I seek in vain.
Even in my dreams he is gone,
    gone, gone.

Oh, if I could but see him again.
See his beloved face, his body
    even if only in my dreams.
If I could hold him again.
It would be such a comfort.
Why is this also denied me?

My dreams are often so real.
If I could at least be with you in my dreams,
    it would be easier to let you go
        in my daily life.

I have not given up the hope.
I will never give up the hope
    of seeing you again
        in my dreams.

6 months

The long cold winter has passed.
The first signs of spring are here.
Tentatively I sit in the sun.

I keep looking around me.
Soon you will notice where I am
    and place your chair beside me
        as you always do.
Together we will bask
    in the spring's first warm rays.

No-one comes.
The terrace remains empty.
The sun goes on shining.
New little green leaves flutter.

It can't be.
There must be some mistake.
Spring cannot come without you.
If you have stopped
    then everything must stop.

The sun goes on shining.
The new green starts appearing everywhere.
I can't bear it.
I want to run and hide.
Bury myself inside
    in the cold of winter.
Make everything stop, stop
    till you come again.

How can everything go on
    as if nothing has happened?
My whole world has ground to a halt.
Yet nature relentlessly blossoms again.

I won't look.
I won't feel.
I ignore the new budding life around me.
For me there is no Spring.
There can be no Spring
    without You.

6 months

Terrified,
   so terrified am I
     of falling back
       into that insecure, ungainly
        young girl
       that I once was.

You so filled me with love
   that I started to radiate
     your warmth
       into my limbs.

So strong, so secure
   did I feel,
     so loved
   that I could blossom out
     and become
       that being
         that I was destined to be.

If I let the realisation
   sink in
     that you are really dead,
   then the threatening wave
     that looms high above me
  will thunder down.
And that being
   that was *you/me*
     will drown.

★

6 months

Once I had a future.
Now there is only the moment
   and how to get through it.

Once we had plans,
   so many plans.
Vacations.
Far-off warm countries.
Grandchildren.
Silently enjoying old age together.

Now there is a total blank.
Everything has come to a screeching halt.

I can only imagine a future
   with you beside me,
   but that is no more.
A future without you is unimaginable.
A future with another
   seems an impossibility.

So there is no future.
Only **now**.
Only the agonising, lonely **now**.

"Living in the now."
Ironic.
Not achieved through
   hours of meditation.
Brought about by
   death,
   separation,
   pain.

✯

7 months

How can I possibly go on alone
    without you?
The one person who accepted me
    as I was.
Loved me for who
    I am.
With all my imperfections.
Because of them... as you so often said.

Your big presence filling up the house.
Warmth, caring, love.
So busy you always were.
So full of life.
Never seeming to tire.
Always knowing where you were going.
Just living alongside you
    that vibrancy rubbed off onto me.
Filled me with a sense of purpose,
    a sense of well-being.

Now you are gone.
I am empty,
    bereft of you,
        of your vitality and love.

As a shadow I move around,
    confused in the darkness.
Crying out in vain
    for you,
    for your presence,
    for your comforting body,
    for your love.
And it does not come.

You don't come any more.
I call and call
   in vain.

I can't stand it.
The pain of it.
The longing
   for what can no longer be.

I want to just
   sink away
     and die.
But I don't die.
I am doomed to go on living
   without you.
It seems such an impossibility.
Every day I am amazed
   that I still live,
   that I go through the motions of living.
How can Kay live without Job?

★

7 months

How have I been able to survive
    these past long months?
Struck down I was.
Paralysed with shock,
    with unbelief.
It could not be true.
Life without you.
My big protector.

Your loving, caring body,
    all around me, in me,
        over me.
Nothing could ever harm me
    while you were there.

You so loved to protect me.
While I basked in your sun.
Yes, you would shine on me
    and I on you.
So we nourished each other
    and grew in each other's
        rays of light.

Now I must go on alone.
Alone in the dark
    without you at my side
        lighting the way.

8 months

My Job, my Job,

I miss you so.

Will I ever dare

to let you go?

8 months

If you could come back
   for one whole month.
Just one month.
Strong and healthy.
   My Job.

How we would savour
   the moments,
     knowing that they would have to last
   an eternity.

We would go off
   and be alone together.
Just you and I.

Nothing could come between us.
   No daily worries,
   no fears.
As we would know
   the greatest fear.
Your death,
   our separation
     was inevitable
and would soon
   be there.

Every moment precious,
   laden with that special harmony,
     that exists between us.

Two beings,
    so different,
    yet somehow
    the one complementing,
        fulfilling the other
            on all levels,
    creating a sense
        of completeness,
        of peace,
        of wanting nothing more in life
            than being together.

8 months

I love you.
I love you.
I love you.
You are dead
    but the love flows on.
How does one stop
    this outpouring of love?

Just because I can't see you any more,
    touch you any more,
        does not mean that I don't feel you any more.
You are still all over,
    all around.

How does one cut the cord
    that binds us?
It is not *one* cord
    but many cords
        that must be cut.

You have become a part of me.
Thus I would be wounding myself so.
And can one cut out love?
How do you do that?

Cover it up with other activities.
Push it deep inside,
    where it will not disturb.
Even this I hesitate to do
    as it is still so beautiful,
        still so alive.
Must I bury it with you?

★

9 months

Oh, my sweet, wonderful Job.
I miss you so.
I miss you so so much.

Can you hear me
    from that place where you are?
Do you visit me
    every now and then?

Can you still feel my love?
Can you rejoice in it
    or is it a burden to you?

☆

9 months – Grindelwald

I look at the waterfall,
   at the glorious mountains
     that once thrilled me so.
Now I feel nothing.

Even though you were not always beside me,
   you were there.
A safe, warm, loving background,
   in which I could relax and Be.
Be open and receptive
   to this God-made beauty.

I look once more
   at the cascading water.
This time it pierces through my numbness
   and I feel **pain**,
     pain, pain.
How can I stand it?
Quickly it moves to close again.
The memory causes the grief to come.
The tears, tears, tears.

See note 3a.

9 months – The message
(Grindelwald – Switzerland)

Our favourite walk
   in these beautiful Alps.
Every step I take.
Everywhere I look
   I see, I hear
      echoes of you.

I feel you
   close beside me.
Your presence so natural
   in this majesty
      of white mountain peaks,
      green alpine slopes,
      fields of brightly coloured flowers.

Total unreality,
   you not being here.
He is here.
He is not here.
My mind cannot grasp,
   cannot encompass the truth.
Where are you?
I am walking in your domain.
How can you *not* be here?

You used to become
   totally alive
      with each stride you took
   along these mountain paths.

Irresistibly drawn
    to our favourite spot.
We used to rest here
    beside this rushing stream.
Sitting close, close,
    on the mossy stones.
Drinking in the sights,
    the smells, the sounds.
Rejoicing
    in being together.
Surrounded by these majestic peaks.

I sit now
    alone.
Remembering.

Suddenly your voice
    rings loud and clear.
Within me?
Around me?
I feel the emotions rise up,
    to choke me,
    to cloud my mind.
I push them away.
I grab my pencil
    and write down your words.

On and on
    You pour out
        your message to me.

What I refused to hear
    before you died
        now flows over me.
The words you dared not utter.
    'The final good-bye'
        you now pronounce
            loud and clear.
With so much love,
    so much compassion,
    so much faith
        in my ability to survive.

You commemorate our love,
    agreeing that love
        overflows the boundary of death.
You give thanks
    to the full life we had together.
You say you will never forget me,
    nor what I meant to you.
You urge me to go on
    without you.
Still bathed in your love
    but without your earthly presence.

You finish with
    "Good-bye...
        till we meet again."

Your voice fades.
I am left in a daze.
Did I really hear him?

My hands grasp
   the written pages
      of my notebook.
I dare not look.

It takes three days
   till I have the courage
      to read what you said.
The tears.
The pain.
The sorrow
   now rise.

Job spoke to me.
I heard him again.
I did not see him.
Yet I know he was there.

Then he must be dead.

For the *first* time
   the emotional reality
      of his death
         starts to sink in.

See note 3b.

9½ months

You mowed the lawn.
You cut the grass.
How I loved to watch
   you move in the garden.
     My man.

Now the grass grows long.
The garden unkempt.
Everyone can see
   my man is no longer.

The wilderness grows
   wild, wild.
Until the day dawns.
The grass must be cut.

The lawn has been mowed.
   Neat, tidy.
Just as beautiful
   as you always did it.

We used to expand together,
   gazing at the wide greenness,
     in admiration,
     in self-delight.

Now I sit alone
   and weep for you.

10 months

Lovely warm summer weather,
   once a joy
      to be relished, treasured,
   is now a torture.

The warmth invites me
   to relax,
   to expand,
   to savour the heavily laden air,
      the smell of the grass,
      the sight of the flowers.

The garden mocks me now.
The place beside me
   screamingly empty.
The warm expansion
   brings only pain.

Together we rejoiced
   in the greenness around us
   in the fact that this spot
      of quiet and peace
         was our private domain.
We had created it,
   watched it grow
      through so many hot summers.
Shared satisfaction, pride.
   "Look how softly the grass grows."
   "Look at the lushness of those flowers."
Silently together we look,
   admire and relish
      the nature around us.

Now the singing birds,
    the warm heavy air,
    the inviting garden around me
      strike chords of pain
        deep inside.
Hollowness, emptiness
    echoes.

I want to run,
    to hide from the warm, hot sun.
Bury myself
    in the dark, cold inside of me.

☆

10 months

Standing in the warm heat of summer
    on the tennis court.
How often, oh how often
    were you not by my side.
Your body moving in anticipation.
Smashing the oncoming ball.

Oh, it felt so good, so good.
Your large male body
    intercepting that ball.
I needed only to give silent support,
    silent admiration
        for your strength,
            your agility,
            your maleness,
            your protection.
You were mine.
We formed a team.

Your silent encouragement
    inspires me
        to pull myself out of my lethargy,
        to hit that ball,
        to move,
        to live,
        to enjoy
            my body,
            our bodies,
            our togetherness.

Together we are strong.
Together we are invincible.
No-one can touch me.
I want to cry out to all:
    "Look we are one, **one**.
    He is mine – I am his."

I glory in our oneness
    in the face of the spectators,
    in the face of all those around us,
        outside of us.
Our silent bond
    of strength, of love.

And now, and now.
The heat is the same.
The red gravel under my feet.
Where must I get the strength from
    to hit that ball
        without your silent loving support?

Like a robot I hit
    missing you with each stroke.
The tears streaming.
The only thing left
    freely flowing.

✯

10 months

You wrote the cheques.
You signed the bills.
You filed the taxes.
You arranged the insurance.

To my amazement
    you loved doing it.
Taking care of everything.
Taking care of us.

Oh Job,
    I miss it so.
Being so well looked after by you.
Not having to think.
Free to float and dream,
    knowing that all has been taken care of.

You revelled in it.
The big provider.
The man,
    protecting, looking after
        his woman.

I so loved being
    cushioned by you
        from all material worries.
Even if it meant being
    'the dependent little woman.'

I loved feeling frail
    next to your strength
        because I knew I was not weak.
As you knew it.

So we played out
    our man-woman roles.
We gloried in it.
The delicate interplay
    enhancing
        our love.

11 months

So unprotected I feel.
With you, I felt so safe.
   Oh, so safe.

No-one could harm me.
Under your wings,
   your protection
I was safe from danger
   real and imagined.

You were so solid,
   so very solid.
Everyone respected you.
No-one would have dared
   to harm me
      in any way imaginable.

Now I feel so exposed,
   so alone in the world.

11 months

I miss you.
I miss you so,
    so, so much.
Words are inadequate
    to describe
        that aching, continuous
            missing.

Friends comfort.
Children support.
But the ache remains.
The agonising
    missing
        of that *one* presence
            that nothing seems able to replace.

The more people around
    the louder the clamour inside
        for you, YOU, **YOU**.

The rebellious denial
    still cries out:
        He can't be gone forever.
        It is not true.
But ever quicker comes the response:
        He is gone, gone, gone.
        Forever.
        That caring, loving presence
            is no more.

☆

11 months

It still remains so incredible,
   so unbelievable,
      that someone so vital,
         so alive,
      is no more.
Someone who filled my life
   so completely
      exists no more.

No more, **no more**.
What do these words mean?
How can a beloved,
   who reaches so deeply
      into all my fibres,
   be no more?

I still hear his voice
   inside of me.
I still see him
   standing, moving, sitting
      around the house
      in the garden.
All over.

No, it is not really him.
But the memory is so strong.
It would be so natural
   for him to be there,
      where I see him
         in my mind's eye.
More normal than
   not to see him.

11½ months

I see us walking
   beside a river in Belgium.
The sun is shining.
All is green and blue around us.
I am contented, happy.

Did I realise that I was happy?
That something so simple
   as the two of us
      being together,
      enjoying the rhythm of the hike,
        of the nature around us,
        of the harmony between us
could end?

That death could put a stop
   to moments like this?
That no more could we sit,
   side by side,
      eating bread and cheese,
      talking,
      staring at the flowing water,
      just being.
Being together.

✮

11½ months

Oh, Job,
you so loved to hike.
Rucksack on your back,
   adventure ahead,
   marching,
   exploring,
   plodding along.
Feeling your body,
   moving,
   so alive.
Enjoying the wide open spaces.
Urging me along.
Trying to convey
   your joy,
   your zest
      in life
   to me.

Oh, I loved to see you so.
   To see you throb with life.
Your zest poured into my veins.
Your energy drove me on.
   Filled me.

I feel so empty now,
   so very empty.
I miss you so completely.

★

11½ months

Sometimes I feel so angry,
 so very angry.
I could smash everything.
Throw bricks through windows.
 Scream and scream.

To what avail
 that fury inside of me?
Nothing can bring him back.
Nothing can restore
 my world
  to the way it once was.

11¾ months

A year ago
   you were still alive.
We spoke about
   my visiting your grave.
Now I do.

But oh, Job,
I did not,
   could not then
      realise what it meant.
I hardly do now.

That warm living body
   now cold
      and decomposing
         in the earth?

My beloved
   reduced to
      bones, sand, worms.
How can one grasp that?
It just is not possible.

✪

1 year

The loss is so great,
   so all encompassing
     that it takes
  weeks and weeks,
  months and months
     to realise what it entails.

Again and again
  comes the realisation:
     This is no more.
     That will never be again.
     That is over forever.

With each realisation
  comes the pain.
     Again and again.

I am left
  weeping,
  devastated,
  powerless,
     so powerless in face of this
      ever widening
    loss.

✵

1 year

I can't bear it one minute longer.
This silent empty house
   without you.

The walls echo emptiness,
   sorrow,
   missing you,
   missing you.

How can I go on
   alone?
What for?
Why bother?

Why bother to clean the house,
   to go shopping?
Why bother?
Why do anything any more?

I just want to
   sink down,
     down, down.
Not think any more.
Not feel any more.
Not be any more.

✭

1 year

It's so final,
   so final.
The **End**.

Never see you again.
Never hear you again.
Never feel you again.
I can't stand it.

The moment I was dreading
   is drawing closer and closer.
The terrible realisation
   that you really and truly
      are gone forever.

1 year

It's such a struggle
   to get up
      out of that warm bed.
It's such a struggle
   to move,
      to keep moving.

My body rebels.
My body is so heavy,
   so heavy with tears,
      with sadness,
      with anger,
      with helplessness.

Keep going.
Keep going.
   I urge.
Such a battle.
Such an uphill struggle.
I don't want to.

I just don't want to
   move,
   continue,
   live.
But I must.
I must try.
Make an effort.
I promised myself.

My heavy body,
My lethargic limbs
    subtly rebel.

Hour after hour
    I drag myself
        around the house.
Desperately hoping
    that the engine,
        the motor
            within me
        will start up again.
That that spark of life
    will flare up
        once more.

1 year

Bitter sweet.
Bitter sweet.
The memories
   of how it was.
Of how we met.
Of how we loved
   and loved.

I hold out my arms
   to embrace,
   to hold.

Only the fragrance
   of what once was
     do I clasp.

The aftertaste
   that lingers
     on the tongue.
After the vintage wine
   has been savoured.

1 year

It is cold.
I wear your pullover.
I can still smell you.

I bury my face in it.
Your chest,
    so warm,
    so broad,
    so comforting.

I love you so.

1 year

I see you sitting opposite me.
   Years and years ago.

Your hand in mine.
Fascinated I gaze
   at the hairs
      on the back of your fingers.

At that moment
   I felt throughout my being
      a knowing:
'You would stand by me.
   A friend.
   A rock.
   Steadfast.
One I could trust
   always.'

Now you are gone,
   gone, gone.
Leaving that image
   dented on my mind.
Mocking me.
Comforting me
Driving me crazy
   with longing
      for that
      which can no longer be.

✩

13 months

Beautiful memories.
Yes, I do have those.
No-one can take them away from me.

Nothing can erase them.
Not even death.

At first I balked
    at having to resort to memories.
No, I wanted him.
    Him.
Alive, vibrating.
I refused to accept
    that it was over,
        gone.
Gone forever.

But here to stay,
    ingrained deep within me,
        are all those memories
            of love, tenderness, life.
No, those can never die.

I am learning.
Yes, learning,
    through tears and pain,
        to be grateful
    that I do have those aching,
        sustaining memories.

'Rebirthing' – 13 months

In a group.
Twenty people.
Deeply breathing.
Loud music.

The rising rumble of noise.
People shouting, screaming.
The air filled
    with flying emotions.

I feel my grief
    rising.

Job, Job.
Where are you?
Come back.
Please, please.

Encouraged by the screams
    around me,
I slowly dare to let
    the agony,
        buried within,
            surface.

Suddenly, it breaks through.
I start to scream
    wildly, uncontrollably.

Oh, it is so good,
    so good.
To scream and scream.
To go deep into the terrible agony.
To throw it out.

I hear myself
    howling like a wolf,
        not human at all.
Can that be me?

I don't care.
I have broken through all my barriers,
    through all my protective walls.
Finally, finally
    I completely let go.

And instead of the dark pit
    of madness
        I am free.
Free
    to express
        that terrible agony
            deep, deep inside of me.

I scream out my anger
    at him.
For leaving me.
My pain in having to let him go.
NO, NO, NO.
    I won't.
    I won't.

I relive those agonising moments
    just before his death.
Now I truly experience the unbelievable anguish.
That terrible conflict:
Desperately wanting him to live,
    yet responding to his last wish
        of dying quickly,
I cut his silver cord,
    his spiritual lifeline.
Oh, the pain,
    the wrenching pain
        of that moment.

Suddenly, I sense
    JOB
        hovering over me.
I hear him say:
    "Dat was je laatste gift aan mij.
    Your last gift of love to me."

My hands start to move
    as of themselves.
They caress his body
    of air,
        floating above me.

I cry and cry
    heartbroken.
He is here.
He is here.
    He is gone forever.

Gently, the music quietens.
The screams lessen.
The emotions subside.

I feel drained
    but filled
        with a sense of peace.
The pus has drained away,
    leaving a clean wound
        that now can heal.

☆

See notes 4, 1a, 1c.

13 months

We met.
We loved.
You died.
But we lived.

Those precious moments
    of deep union
        we experienced.

So many have never felt
    what we felt.
Gone now... yes,
But once there.

That deep throbbing.
That openness.
That surrender
    to an all encompassing feeling.
That closeness.
That sublime intimacy.
We had it all.
    Yes, Yes.

Nothing can erase
    those deeply ingrained
        memories.

Be grateful, Kay.
Give thanks
    that you once had it all.

If now the pain
    is stronger,
      more agonising.

It was worth it.
I lived.

13 months

Oh, to feel
   arms around me again.
To be close.
To feel the soft warmth
   of another.

The longing.
The yearning
   goes so deep,
     becomes unbearable.

Yet, at the touch
   of another
     comes the weeping,
       the sorrow.
The deep terrible
   sorrow.

13 months

Starting to feel
   the children again;
      their warmth,
      their loving,
      their caring,
      their giving.

At first it was as a drop
   in an ocean of despair.
Now it is a glow
   of warmth,
   of fragile belonging,

At first I rebelled
   at having to rely
      on independent young beings,
   just starting to spread their wings,
      leaving the nest.

Now I am learning to relax.
Learning to receive,
   where before I could only give.
Feeling blessed
   in their sweet attempts
      to show:
"Mama, *we* are still alive.
      We care for you.
      We love you.
      We need and want
         You
      to be alive!"

★

13 months

Yes, I still
    miss you so much.
Love you and miss you.

Only now,
    the pain of missing you
        is held at arm's length
    while I struggle
        to live again.

The realisation
    that I am alone
        without you
    remains on the surface.
It does not sink so deep.

I consciously let it remain there
    so that I am free
        to pull myself together
    in order to function.
In order to slowly,
    step by step
        orientate myself
    in this world
        without you.

★

13 months

At night I am starting
   to dream about you again.
Dreams in which you are still alive.
Dreams in which I know
   you are going to die.

Now, I fully realise how precious
   our last months and days together were.
I want to make time
   stand still.
Draw out the moments.
Record the 'I love you's
   again and again.
Trying to indent them
   on my mind,
   in my memory
     forever.

☆

14 months

Two dreams I had last night:

A boy sits beside a huge wall.
The wall starts to crumble.
The boy does not move.
I think: "He will be killed!"

The wall falls the other way.
I hear a voice say:
    "It was not his time, Kay."

Job and I are together somewhere.
He says: "I want to go home."
I say: "I want to stay a while."
    He goes.
    I stay.

A realisation deep in me.
That's life and death, Kay.
He wanted to go home.
I wanted to stay
    a while longer.

14 months

In an aeroplane,
   high, high,
      up in the sky.
The clouds like soft cotton-wool
   below me.
The sun's rays shedding
   a soft mysterious glow.
Breathtakingly beautiful.

Is this the landscape,
   wherein you now float,
      dream and exist?
The wide expansiveness,
   you so loved
      on earth
Your daily surroundings?

Oh, Job, Job,
   if only I could share it all
      with you
   as we once did.

Now I can only speculate.
Intuitively feel
   your presence,
   your voice,
   your messages.
Your present existence,
   so achingly near,
   yet so far away.

14 months

Walking along the beach
   in the Algarve.
I see a white haired couple,
   holding hands.

I remember how in the past,
   we knowingly smiled at each other;

Seeing *ourselves*
   in the distant future.
Basking in the warmth of the prospect
   of growing old together.
Sharing the same memories,
     the same children,
     the same grandchildren.
Looking back on a life together,
   with satisfaction, pride
     and love.

Oh, it was such a deliciously
   comfortable feeling
     of well being,
     of intimate trust,
     of warmth.

Shared dreams.
Shattered by fate,
   turned into dust,
     bones and earth.

Gone, gone.
All gone.

Unimaginable
   Me
growing old
    without you.

14 months

I wanted to see you grow old.
I was waiting for the first grey
   to appear on your temples.

Now I will never see it.
Never see you in your armchair,
   growing old and mellow.
While I indulgently
   feast my eyes on you.
While I sink away.
Luxuriating in the cosy comfortableness
   of growing old,
      together with you.

☆

14 months

Every time
    beauty touches me,
    truth touches me,
    nature,
    music.
The tears flow.

That layer,
    deep within,
        belongs to you.

14 months

Waking up.
Sunday morning
   used to be so peaceful.
The day stretching deliciously ahead.
You lying beside me,
   warm, close.

I don't have to do anything.
I can just *be*,
   sink away,
   drift away
      into myself.
I feel so peaceful,
   so contented.
Life lazily stretches ahead.

Now, if I let go,
   if I drift away
      into myself,
   if I go too deep
I touch the pain,
   the emptiness,
   the futility of it all.

So I am active,
   I plan,
   I do,
Anything, anything
   to cover up
      that aching black hole
      deep, deep
         within me.

✭

15 months

To feel my own strength.
My own strength
   flowing in my veins.
Free of him,
   flowing,
   strong,
   good.

Resistance.
I don't want to be free.
And yet
   at times
   it does flow.
My *own* strength.

15 months

Struggling like a baby
   to take her first steps
     alone.
Looking around
   with fresh eyes
     at this new world.

Balanced precariously
   on her own two feet.
For the first time
   in a long time.

Can I make it?
I am going to fall.
   I do.
Again and again.

Yet each time
   I stand up once more.
Something in me
   pushes me on,
   urges me to rise,
   to take the next few steps
     out into this new unknown world.

☆

15 months

Days go by,
    when I don't think of you.
Enjoying a new-found
    freedom.
Getting on with life,
    with living.

Then suddenly it strikes again,
    piercing through
        all those protective walls
            I have so carefully built.

The wound
    aches and pains
    and cries out
        for you.

I let the storm
    of protest
        rage on
    till it quietly dies.
The longing
        for you
    safely buried
        once more
    beneath the sands
        of self-comfort,
so carefully nurtured.

☆

15 months

Yes, there are times
   when I don't think of you.
When I am intensely occupied
   with some activity.
Involved with another person.
Distracted away from feelings
   about you.

To my amazement
   I feel
      joy,
         life,
            flowing
            through my veins once more.

Till some stray thought
   or memory
   and any deep emotion
      touches upon
      that well of grief
         waiting to bubble up again.

✿

15 months

Job, your grandson was born today.
Your first grandchild.
    And you are not here to hold him.

How we looked forward to this moment.
How you longed to have
    a little one on your lap again.

I loved to watch you
    play and hold
        the children of the neighbourhood.
One day, our looks used to say,
    it will be one of ours.

Now that day is here
    but you are gone.

Yet still I see
    in my mind's eye
You holding little Klaas,
    tenderly, lovingly,
        so proud of your daughter.

Try as I can
    that image does not leave me.
It is indented on my mind,
    haunting me.
Trying to impress
    its reality
        above the stark unrelenting truth
          of your blatant absence.

★

15 months

Looking at your photo.
You smiling at me.
You seem so real,
    so alive.

For a split second
    I think:
'This is all a dream.
I will wake up.
You will still be here
    with me.
Alive and well.'

I feel confused.
What is reality?
What is a dream?

The voice that says:
'No, Kay, stop this now,'
or the voice that says:
'Soon I will wake up
    and feel and see
    Job sleeping peacefully
        beside me'?

★

15 months

Such a fragile thin line:

Enjoying the freedom
    of being alone.
Doing what I want
    when I want to.
Peaceful, calm.
Floating along
    free.

The fragile line
    quivers,
    turns,
    cries.

I did not ask for
    freedom.
Where is the warmth,
    the closeness,
    the intimacy
of days gone by?

But, dear Kay,
    you are living now.
Now you are *free*.
Welcome this new state.
    This gift.
For it shall enable you
    to grow,
    to strengthen yourself,
    to shine from within.

16 months (1)

It's all coming back again.
The terrible, terrible
   missing
      of him.

I thought I was over
   the worst of it.
It felt better,
   liveable.

Now it is as if I am going
   deeper,
      deeper into myself.
Daring to face,
   really face
      the future
         without him.

I can't.
I won't
   but I must.
I must.

I long for the day
   when it is all over.
When I too will die.
When I can give up
   this never-ending struggle.

Oh, the peace,
the peace of it.
It beckons to me
across the universe.
Soothingly, comfortingly.
Then it will be over.
All over.
Infinite peace.

Oh, Kay.
Please try.
You still have so much.
So much.
Hang on there
for a while longer.

16 months (2)

Going deeper,
  ever deeper
    into the dark recesses
      of my mind.

I find this lonely abandoned child.
  Crying out
    in anguish,
    helplessly,
  not comprehending
    what has hit her.

Please help me.
  Help me.
I am drowning
  in sorrow,
  in heaviness,
  in aloneness.

☆

16 months (3)

A child
  crying
    for her Daddy.

Please come.
Please, please
  come back.

Make it better
  again.
The pain.
The awful pain.

Take me in your arms.
Let me sink away
  into that wonderful
    all encompassing protection
      of your big safe body.

Oh, Daddy, Daddy,
  where are you?
You can't leave me
  alone like this.

You promised.
You promised me.

★

16 months (4)

The infinite
  aloneness
    of man.

Just one person
  lies between
    that aching
      abandoned,
        aloneness

and the
  all encompassing
    warmth
      of belonging,
      of oneness.

★

16 months

Nothing fills the hole
   left by you.

I try.
I really try.
Loving children.
Warm friends.
Satisfying work
   temporarily fill the gap.
But when they are gone.
When the work is done.
Emptiness screams out to me.

I know I must learn
   to fill that gap
     with myself.
But it is so hard,
   so terribly difficult.

Is this the lesson
   I must learn?

16 months

K. 1.:   Would you give up
        your new independence
        your freedom
    for those caring loving arms
        around you?

K. 2.:   But I never had the choice.
    It was rudely thrust on me.
    I never asked for it:
        The independence.
        The feeling of confidence.
        Being able to stand alone.
        Make my own decisions.
        Do what I want
           when I want to.

K.1.:   Would you ever
        willingly, freely
           have given up
        that all encompassing
           love and protection?

K. 2.:   No, never!

K.1.:   So, how else
        could you have learnt
        that you can stand
           on your own feet
             alone,
        relying only
           on your inner resources?

K.2.: Still I rebel.
        But one day
          I will accept
            that this is what
          I had to learn.

⭐

16 months

I so so long
    for your arms
        around me,
        holding me.
Telling me:
    It is all over.
    The nightmare
        is over.

I relax
    in your arms.
I let go
    the sorrow,
    the pain,
    the aloneness.
I sink away
    once more
        into you.

Oh, the bliss
    of not having
        to think any more.
Just feel
    your strong loving arms
        around me.
Knowing
    you will take care
        of me
           forever.

★

17 months

Playing golf.
Seeing Job everywhere.
Missing him.
The ache castes a pall
    on this lovely warm spring day.

Oh, Kay, Kay,
    why not enjoy
        the sun,
        the soft breeze,
        the movement of my own body?

I feel strong.
I feel alive.

Cast off the ropes that bind.
    The ropes of the past.
Step out
    of your cage of sorrow.
Recognise
    your freedom
        to *BE*
        to feel
        to live
            once more.

☆

17 months

Still bleeding.
    Still feeling
        like a wounded animal
           without you.

The pain does not go away.
It goes deeper.
It is becoming more real.

In a way
    you are coming closer again.
I am letting the *dead you*
    come close.

You walk beside me
    in the streets.
You whisper in my ear.
I hear you constantly
    encouraging me
        to go on.

At the sound of your voice
    the tears come,
    the pain.
The realisation
    that I can't touch you,
        hold you,
        feel your arms around me.
I can only hear you.

I now can allow myself
   to feel
      your voice,
      your presence.
It is painful
   but it comforts.

A part of you
   lives on
      in me.

                    ☆

                   125

17 months

A miracle.
Sometimes it feels like a miracle
    that I lived with you
      for so long,
    that you cared for me,
    that you loved me.

That I loved
    and enjoyed you
      so deeply.

Was it real
    or a young girl's longings?

Sometimes I feel so confused.
Who am I?
The girl from long ago
    waiting for her knight in shining armour?

That girl keeps coming forward
    amazed that her dreams
      have become reality...

... only to realise
      that her knight was snatched away
        before she fully realised
          what a miracle he was.

17 months

You are mine.
I am yours.
An inescapable reality.
You are locked
    deep within my heart.
The key is lost.
Deep within
    you shall always remain.

Love song AD 1200

Dû bist mîn.
Ich bin dîn.
Des sollst dû gewiss sîn.
Dû bist beslozzen
    in mînem herzen.
Verlorn ist das slüzzelîn.
Dû muost immer darinne sîn.

See note 5.

127

17 months

Every month
　　come the deposits,
　　the pension money,
　　the insurances.

You worked so hard
　　for so long.
Yet now you are not here
　　to enjoy the rewards.

So responsible you were.
All those years
　　taking care of us all.

Even now
　　when you are gone
　　the reminders
　　　　flow in.

All the plans
　　you had.
What we would do
　　when you stopped working,
　　when you would start to enjoy
　　　　the fruits of those years of hard work.

Yet now,
　　now you are gone
　　　　and it is I
　　who must enjoy
　　　　for you.

Will I ever
　　really be able to?

1½ years

In those moments
    when I don't linger
        on days gone by,
        on what could have been,
        on my yearning for intimacy,
    life is good.

I can do what I want to
    when I want to.
I am free
    to do as I please.

I enjoy the sun.
The pulsing of nature
    all around me.
The movements of my body.
The love of my children.
The warmth of friends.

I feel so much better
    than a year ago.
Will time really heal all wounds?

1½ years

Kay,
    It is better to have loved
       and lost,
       than not to have loved at all.
    It is better to feel pain
       than nothing at all.

You are on earth
    to live,
    to feel,
    to learn.

Don't stop feeling.
Remain open
    to the pain of your loss
    and you will feel
       the joy of being alive.

Why else are you on earth?
Why else did you leave
    that place of dreamy contentedness,
but to feel that
    despite the worst
       that you could imagine:
          the loss of
       sheltered, caring mutual love

    You still ARE.

Make the most
　　of what is left.
Try to live each moment
　　　for what it is,
　　　not what it was
　　　or could have been.

This moment, call out
　　　not *I was*,
　　　not *I will be*
　　　　but I AM.

1½ years

Oh, it is so good,
   so good
      to feel my inner strength
         once more.

I was so shattered.
My world disintegrating around me
   that I lost all grip
      on my innate ability:
         to survive,
         to BE,
         to continue.
  To feel the link
     with my source,
     with Life,
     with meaning,
     with the joy
        of being alive.

✮

1½ years

Emerging from
    a dark tunnel.

While within
    I could not imagine
        it would ever end.

I was told
    over and over:
There would be light
    on the other side.
But I remained
    inconsolable
        in my disbelief.

Now I see the light.
It is different,
    very different
        from the light
            I left behind.

But, yes,
    light there is
    shining in front of me.

✪

1½ years

At rest.
Peace.
Finally peace
   from wild emotions
      of love,
      of loss,
      of pain,
      of grief.

At peace.
Finally at peace
   after years
      of activity,
   of having to go somewhere,
   of having to experience something,
   of having to do.

Blissfully peaceful.
I have experienced it all.
I don't need to go anywhere,
   be anything
      but what I am now.

Yes, I can finally rest.
I can cherish the past.
I can nourish and integrate it
   and peacefully discover
      who I am now.

★

134

1½ years

I don't need to go
    anywhere, any more.
I have already been there.
Now I can just rest
and *BE*.

1½ years

Sitting enjoying
   without you.
Enjoying things I never used to
   before.

Before things had meaning
   in terms of You.
Being with you.
Sharing with you.

Activities in which you had no part,
   which could not be shared later
   were without meaning.
To be quickly rushed through.
To be avoided.

Now, now everything has changed.
Everything is meaningless.
Thus every thing acquires a meaning
   in itself.
There is no life without you.
Yet, every minute is Life.

As the urge to live
   reawakens in me,
I discover that
   every small thing,
   every tiny activity
      vibrates with its own life.

To my amazement
   I enjoy that
      which before I shunned.

There is a new peace in me.
I don't have to rush
   to have those precious moments
      with you.
I can just *BE*
   and calmly take in all around me.
Open myself to this
   strange world
      in which you have no part.

By organising my life
   around you
There was so much
   I did not see.

Every day I discover
   a new aspect
      of that life that faintly blinked
         outside of our orbit.
Outside of you and me.

To my amazement
   it is not as dull and joyless
      as I once thought it to be.

☆

1½ years

Flow with the tide.
   Just *BE*.
Accept my grief.
Flow with what is
   NOW.
Don't resist.
Energy lost.
Feel the expansion
   if I let go
      expectations
   and just
      am.

✯

19 months

You visit me
    every now and then.

Is it really you,
    your soul
or my longing
    for contact with you?

Sometimes it is as if
    you have never left me.
Your voice
    encourages me,
    soothes me,
    caresses me,
    smiles benignly
        down on me.

I don't really feel alone.
Not even after one and a half years.
For you are there
    always when I need you.

I don't care
    whether it really is you.
It feels the same.
I love you so
    my Job.
Even now.

19 months

Looking at a film.
Seeing two lovers reunite.
The tears well up.

Imagine if I were to meet him again.
Now – after one and a half years!
He would take me in his arms:
    "The separation is over, Kay.
    The nightmare has past.
    I am back.
    I will stay with you
        always.
            Forever."

Oh, the wonder of it.
Feeling his love,
    his protection,
        once more.
Healing all wounds.

As the image
    dims and fades,
I hear his voice
    echoing around me:

"But I *am* here, Kaytje.
I have not left you,
    not completely.
I see your sorrow,
    your tears,
only you don't see me.
You will.
You will."

✦

19 months

For days and days
   I feel good.
Free of sorrow.
Free of memories.
I can live again.

Then I do too much.
I become tired,
   exhausted.
And it starts to seep through once more.

That paralysed feeling
   of hopelessness,
   of heaviness,
   of going nowhere.

I thought it was over
   but it is here again.
Feeling bereft of you
   instead of feeling free.
Feeling drained
   instead of bubbling over
     with life.
Not wanting to go on
   instead of waiting eagerly
     for life's next move.

Oh, will it ever end;
having to periodically feel
   this gaping hole
     within?

✮

19 months

Starting to feel 'woman' again.
Allowing myself
   to feel 'woman' again.

You are not here.
I must go on alone.
I am a woman.
My man – You
   deserted me.
Not purposely – No.
But you are not here
   to be my other half.

My other half
   I won't find again.
But my woman's
   desires and impulses
     need a man.

19 months

You left me.
I start to feel
    anger.
For the first time
    real anger.
I am reduced
    to seeking warmth elsewhere.

My body cries out
    for intimacy,
    for warmth,
    for the touch of another.
And you are no longer here.
I know you would have understood
    my need.
You understood me so well.

However, it is *you*
    I want.
The anger wells up.
How dare you leave me
    exposed like this?
How could you?
You, who were always so protective
    of your Kaytje.

19 months

What of the craving
   to be touched
      by a man?
I am not ready but
   my body is.
My body never stopped
   craving
      for the warmth
         of another.

Confusion:
   other bodies
      are not yours.

If I give way
   to my body,
      on one level,
         there is desire lulled.
But the ache
   only grows stronger
      for that deeper contact
         on another level.

And for that
   I am not ready.

IMPASSE.

★

20 months

Driving to a weekend course
    where we often went together.
I feel your presence
    gently wafting around me.
'You are not alone
    Kaytje,
I am with you'.
A warm comforting feeling.

Yes, occasionally
    I am able to relish
      'his presence'
    without agonising
    at the loss
      of his 'Being'.

✫

20 months

Dancing wildly
   to African music.
Celebrating life.
Letting my body flow
   in its own wild rhythm.

Suddenly I sense him before me.
   Not his earthly body
      but his *presence*.
The shock of it
   brings the tears,
      the sorrow,
        the terrible loss of him.

My longing grows unbearable.
I stretch out my arms
   to encompass his presence.
I hear him say:
"Goed zo Kaytje,
Ga zo door."

My grief explodes.
So near,
   yet so far,
      so unreachable.

Lying down.
Resting.
Listening to the sounds of a flute.
Its haunting, unearthly melody
    sends me far out.
I feel myself drawn
    Up, up, up...
        ...to where he is.

Wide open spaces.
Unearthly colours.
I rejoice in what I sense and feel:
    He has come into himself.
    So strong and vulnerable.
    So delicately powerful and free.
Words fail to describe
    this place
    or what he has become.

Once more I feel his words
    ring through me:
        "I will tell you all
        as you will tell me all
        when we meet again
        in the far-distant future."

Vibrating with the feel of him.
Saddened, but at peace
    I return to reality.

See note 6.

20 months

Regrets, regrets.
I was often so immensely proud of you.
Why did I not tell you?

So many people praised you.
I felt I should not.
Why?
Maybe you wanted to hear it
    from *me*.

Now, I will never know.

20 months

My Job,
you died
   nearly two years ago.
Yet part of you
   remained behind
   with me
     in our house,
     in our garden,
     in our bed.

Yet now,
     now
   you seem to be slipping away
     from this house
       of which you were
       so much a part.

Even after you were gone
   you breathed life
     into its walls.
Yet now,
     now
   that life's breath
     is gradually decreasing.
The walls start to echo
   silence,
   emptiness.
The garden
   is desolate.

The reality of your absence
   penetrates
      yet another layer,
        deeper,
        deeper.
Till escape
   no longer seems possible.

★

20 months

I miss you so desperately.

The pain
　of having to face
　　your *absolute* absence,
　that *never ever again*
is too excruciating.

It goes underground
　leaving an emptiness,
　a non-feeling,
　a depression,
　a hole.

20 months

Betrayed, deserted, abandoned,
     alone.
Of course,
     you did not do it on purpose.
And yet,
     you left me to fend for myself.
Open, vulnerable.

I trusted you
     to look after me,
     to share my life,
     to share my love.
Together, together
     we would face the future:
          the sorrows, the pain, the joy.

Anger bubbles up.
How could you?
How could you
     leave me behind?

Anger makes me strong.
Anger makes me hard.
I will show you.
I will survive
     without you!

★

20 months

It's back again.
The pain.
The nothingness.

Vacation.
Supposedly delicious days
    of lazy enjoyment.

I drag myself
    through the house
        feeling awful, awful.
Empty, drained,
    paralysed.

A black, dark hole.
Sinking, sinking away.
Numbly, reaching out
    for help.

In vain.
No-one.
No-one
    can fill
        that gaping hole.

★

20 months

I am drowning,
   drowning
      in a sea of grief,
         of emptiness,
         of desertion.

I grasp at anything, anything
   to keep me afloat,
   to keep me alive.
I do things unimaginable before,
   unimaginable after.
Anything, anything
   not to be swallowed up
      in this black hole
         of desperation,
         of nothingness.

☆

Grindelwald (1) – 1¾ years

Why do I continuously
   confront myself so?
Why must I return alone
   to these same Alps,
     where, two years ago,
     we still hiked?

Why force myself to face
   this excruciating pain,
     again and again?

I am drawn to it,
   trying to recapture
     some of the magic
      of how it was
      before he died.

Simultaneously,
   I want to exorcise it
     out of my pores,
     out of my cells
  so that I can go on,
     free, free
      of all these hidden
      memories of pain.

✪

Grindelwald (2) – 1¾ years

Will you walk with me
   my Job
      through these Alpine meadows?
Will you enjoy with me
   my Job
      this moment of rest,
     while I soak in
       the grandeur of these snowy peaks?

My Job, my Job,
   I miss you so.
Each step I take,
   an echo
      of years gone by,
     when we happily
       moved together over these slopes.
Harmony and contentment
   oozing out of our pores
     as we drink in
       the splendour around us.

Kay, he is not here, not here.

With each solitary step
   the truth swirls around me.
The incredible snowy peaks remain
   glistening in the bright sun
     of NOW,
   majestically declaring:
     "We remain, we remain
     while He is no more."

✮

Grindelwald (3) – 1¾ years

I sit high, high up in the mountains.
The most incredible snowy peaks
   panoramically displayed before my eyes.

So many, many times
   in the past
I felt your large body beside me
   as we gazed in wonder
      at this magnificence before us.

Oh, Job, Job.
Where are you now?
Do you also see this
   from another dimension?

I cannot conceive
   of you not being here
      in some form or other.
You, who so delighted
   in the majesty of these pristine peaks.

You would not
   could not
   miss the opportunity
      of once more
      feasting your eyes
         on this splendour,
      of sharing this moment
         with me.

If only I could be sure
    that it is possible
        to drift through the spheres,
    that this comforting presence
        I so often feel
            is really you.

☆

1¾ years – The second message
(Grindelwald – Switzerland)

Once more I find myself on our favourite mountain path.
　　With awe I near 'our' stream.

Will he speak to me again
　　like he did last year?
Will he descend
　　from wherever he is?
Will I hear him again?

I sit down on that mossy rock
　　where we so often sat.

Instantaneously it bursts out
　　all over me.
Dazzling me
　　with its strength,
　　with its force.
Pouring over me
　　like a shower.
His flow of words.
Soothingly, comfortingly,
　　on and on.
Without thinking,
　　my tears freely flowing,
I grasp my pen
　　to capture once again his precious words.

His words of encouragement.
His words of love for me.
His advice.

I should not isolate myself too much.
I should not take life too seriously.
Life is just a game.
A preparation for what comes after.
He will explain it all to me 'later'.

I have powerful helpers
   who are pushing me through:
"Listen to your own intuition.
It is often their voices
   trying to guide you."

He describes where he now is:
"It is lovely here, Kay,
   You know.
   You have been here before.
I am with you all often.

"When you feel me
   I am usually there.
We make the rules here.
I love to follow you all
   every once in a while
      but I have a full existence here.

"We will exchange news
   one day,
      my Kaytje.
It hurts, I know.
Earthly hurt.
Up here, it all makes sense.
It is so peaceful.
The wide open spaces I longed for on earth.
They are here.
Peace, harmony, love."

He gives me advice
   on a problem I am battling with:
"You can't really do any harm.
   Not to yourself.
   Not to another.
Our intrinsic Self
   remains untouched.
It just gets filled and enriched
   with experience,
   with knowledge,
   with love.
Yes, especially with Love.
Love is all.
Love is the fabric of the universe."

He intersperses his 'newly found' wisdom
   with jokes about himself
   and with personal messages.

He ends with:
"Dag lief Kaytje.
Life is life
   and flows
   just like this stream.
All is inevitable.
Try to enjoy
   the fullness around you.
Don't be sad.
Cry ... yes
   but don't be sad.

"Tot de volgende keer
   langs deze beek?"

His message ends.
I feel so good, so good.
So filled with him once more.
I turn away
    from our enchanted spot.
Light-headed.

Blissfully,
    I proceed with my descent
    my climb down this mountain.
This path of Life,
    strewn with rocks and other obstacles,
    opening out unexpectedly
        but hopefully
    into the most beautiful, mystical vistas.

☆

Grindelwald (5) – 1¾ years

Having received Job's message.
I continue down the mountain.
My world seems lighter,
    more playful.
The mountains glisten and shine
    with a mystical quality.

Everything falls into place,
    has meaning,
    makes sense.

A joyous liquid
    gently flows
    through my being.

Non-thinking.
Expanding.
Pores open.
Absorbing.
Just being.
Alive.

☆

Grindelwald (6) – 1¾ years

My Job,
   my Job.
So strange,
   so strange.
This new strength.
This new energy I feel.

It is as if your endurance
   flows through my body now,
   making me strong,
      where before I was weak.

As I stride with ease
   along these mountain paths
I feel your lust for life
   pulsing through my veins,
   urging me forwards.

Not only your strength
   but habits of yours,
   likes and dislikes.
Unnoticed at first
   but ever stronger
      are becoming a part of me.
So many things I used to disdain
   I now relish.

Is it really possible
   that a part of you
      is living on through me?

1¾ years

Moving cosily in my own rhythm.
Contented in a new found peace.

I experience a few days
    of warm deep friendship.
      Shared close intimate moments.

Unnoticed the wound opens.
That place of deep feeling
    of pulsing vulnerability
        that was once open to Job.
Cries out in pain
    when touched
        by someone else.
Opening up
    the newly healed wound.

The blood which had congealed
    starts to flow again.

The pain of it.
I can't stand it.
Not any more.
I thought the agony
    was over
        over.

Quickly Kay, close it.
Please, please
    close it again.

I pull myself together.
Do all those comforting active things
    that I know will thrust me forward,
Away, away
    from this terrible ache inside.

And yes,
    one day, two days.
It is closing, closing.
Clang – it is closed.

Relieved
    so relieved,
I roll gently back into
    my newly found rhythm of peace.

✫

22 months

Meeting someone else,
   who is kind and warm.
A longing reawakens within.
Something in me is aroused
   and starts to lead its own life.

Till it is dashed to pieces
   on the rocks of:
      How to react?
      He is not Job.
      He is not available.

The pain starts to throb again.
I try to push it all away.
To find the peace
   of nothingness again.

✸

22 months

I want
I don't want.
It was always sacred somehow.
Now I must come down to earth.

22 months

Getting closer
   to someone else.

At first the joy
   at the touch
      of another.
The warmth.
The intimacy.

But then the agony starts.

It's not him.
It's not him.
I want him.
The old longings
   start to throb
      through my body.
The memories.

I want to bury myself
   in him,
      him.
No-one else.

Oh, Kay,
   when will it sink in?
He is gone,
   gone.
Forever.

Let GO.
Please.

22 months

Hands, hands,
   but not your hands.
A body pressing against mine.
It feels like yours.
Only it is not yours.
Oh God, oh God.
   Let it be your body.
Please, please.
If only it were your body,
   your hand.

I try to make believe.
   Your touch.
     You.
The tears start pouring.
   But it's not you.
     Not you.

I can't bear it.
But I do.
I must.
Life goes on
   without you.
But why, oh why
   can't it be You
     touching me?

Will I ever be able
   to accept
     the unbearable closeness
       of another?

22 months

Go away.
Go away.

Don't you dare touch me.
I can't stand it.

You feel like him
    but you are not him.
Go away.

You can't love me.
Only he can really love me,
    know me.

It is an illusion.

Confusion.
Turmoil.
Anguish.

What to do.
What to do?

I want to feel love again.
But I can't stand it.

Not again.
Not again.

The fear.
The pain.
The loss.

22 months

Another man.
Holding me.
Threatening to go deeper,
    to come closer,
        really close.

My whole body
    rebels
        in protest.

NO, NO, NO.
I can't.
Betrayal.
I am betraying
    you.

Our last conversation
    suddenly looms up.
I told you there would be other men
    but no-one
        no-one would ever
            occupy the place you held.

Yet now,
    now
someone is threatening,
    trying to penetrate
        that place
    reserved only for you.

I hear your voice:
  "Kaytje, lief Kaytje,
  I am so far away,
    so far away now."

Confusion.
Sorrow.
Tears.

What must I do?

Just let it be.
Don't resist.
Just flow.
Let life take its course.

23 months

Seeing you,
   glimpsing you
      tantalising
         in the children.

It is you.
It is not you.

Happiness.
Grief.
Love.

✩

23 months

Passing your photo.
Pausing for that pang of emotion.
   Nothing.

"You've cried so much, Kay.
It does not help.
He has not come back.
He will not come back."
   Emptiness.

The last link;
   my wild grief
      is fading,
         has been pushed down
            far away inside of me.

Barren.
Forsaken.
Depression.

"Come on, Kay.
   Come on.
   Move.
Life is still
   flowing.
Forget,
   forget
      that abandoned feeling.
Move forward.
One slow step at a time
   into life's main stream
      once more."

☆

23 months

I can choose
    which layer to feel.

The deep one within
    of pain, loss and sorrow

Or the more recent layers,
    covering those deep ones,
        containing other emotions,
          different feelings.
Maybe not so deep
    but distracting,
      enjoyable,
      human,
      good.

★

23 months

I am grateful.
Yes, I am grateful.
I still have so much:
  - good health
  - loving children
  - sweet faithful dog
  - satisfying work
  - loyal friends
  - supportive neighbours
  - enough wealth
  - lovely house
  - green leafy garden.

So many have so little.
I have so much.
Still so much.
How can I want more,
    cling to that which no longer is?

I then deny
    the bounty,
    the abundance
        that still is mine.

⭐

177

23 months

I have cried, wept and sobbed
   so much
      these past two years.
It is as if all my tears
   have finally been shed.

Now, when I feel the tears welling up,
   as a memory pierces through,
      comes the flash:
   "I have experienced this before,
      over and over.
   I have felt the depth of this sorrow.
   It does not bring him back.
   He is dead."

Yes, finally I start to accept
   this fact:
My Job is really dead.

No amount of tears,
   of disbelief,
   of denial
      seems to be able to bring him back
        to me.

This thought
   dries my tears
      before they fall.

I smile in amazement
   at myself.
In wonder.

Is that immense well of tears,
    of sorrow,
finally evaporating?

Two years

When you died
    I felt
        'I can't live without you.
        I can't be happy without you.'

Now two years later
    I realise
        I have lived
            for days and days,
            months and months,
            even years without you.

The past years prove
    I have survived.
Something in me
    wants to deny it,
    wants to cling to my sorrow,
        my last palpable link with you.

Yet, I can no longer deny:
    I *am living* again.
I am starting a new life
    without you by my side.
Incredible as it seems,
    I am succeeding!

★

Two years

Two years, Job.
I can't believe
   I survived two years
     without you!

Two years
   in this empty house.
Two years
   of not feeling your touch,
     your support,
     your love.

Two years
   of not living through you.
Two years
   of uphill struggle
     to find myself.

Two years
   of discovering
     'who is Kay without Job'.

Yes, who is Kay
   without Job?
Whom can Kay love
   but you?
Whom can Kay give to
   but you?

Yet the seed is sprouting.
The bud is growing.
Kay is emerging.
I am discovering
   that I can love others
      besides you.
Give to others.
Be of value to others.

And most difficult of all.
I am starting to live for myself
   and not only through you.

Two years

The two selves of Kay:

The emotional one,
    often in complete chaos.
Threatening to drown
    in the pain, sorrow and agony
        of her loss.

The wise one,
    detached and gently smiling.
Knowing that all will ultimately be well.
Strong and compassionate.
Intuitively guiding
    the emotional one.

Together they form a bond.
Leading each other
    through each new challenge,
        here on this planet earth.

★

Reliving his death yet again – two years later

Completely helpless
I stand by
    while that strong, warm, responding body
        every day grows weaker, frailer,
        slowly withdrawing beyond my reach.
Until finally, lying next to him,
    the withdrawal is complete.
The body no longer responds.

That big warm body
    grows colder and colder.
That body that gave so much comfort
    slowly turns into unresponsive coldness.

My emotional self refuses to perceive
    the cold hardness.
I warm his body
    with my body.

It just is not possible
    that all that is left
        of that strength, that warmth,
           that comforting softness
    is this unresponsive cold hardness I feel.

For nearly two years
    I never allowed that cold dead corpse
        to penetrate my awareness.
NO, I lay next to a body, still warm.
I felt his 'living soul' close by.

His body in the open coffin in our bedroom
    was a comforting presence
        that I did not hesitate to touch
            to feel those familiar hairs on his chest.
I assured myself
    He is still here
        with me.

The cold hardness.
The final withdrawal.
The desertion
    I locked away,
        imprisoned within me.
Until I was strong enough
    to face
        this merciless, terrible, cruel
            Reality.

See note 1c.

Two years

Only now after two years
    can I once more listen to classical music.

The music touches a quivering chord
    that cuts through all barriers,
    reaching deep inside of me,
    touching that place
        of grief, pain and bliss.

I become aware
    of my aloneness.
    Of that connectedness to the other,
        that no longer is.
    Of the inability to feel bliss
        without that pang
            of pain, of nostalgia.
    Of the haunting feeling
        that the reason for my being ceases to exist
            if I no longer move in unison,
        sharing these deeply felt moments
            with that *one other*.

The music relentlessly
    pierces through
        touching chords,
        aching places,
        loving memories.

However, now that time has passed
    I can bear the pain,
    the heart-rending *Reality*:
        It is over.
        Gone forever.

Alone am I
   to face the challenge
      of finding Life's meaning
         without that deep connectedness
            to another.
To find it
   within
      my Self.
To learn
   to breathe
   to walk
   to enjoy
   to BE
for its own sake
   and not by sharing it
      with a beloved.

✮

Two years

I indulged myself,
    spoiled myself,
    pampered myself.
There was no-one else to do it but me.

I let myself cry,
    scream,
    sink deep into nothingness.
I tried not to judge
    my strange behaviour.
I let myself *be*
    as I was.

Now, out of that pitiful mess
    is emerging
        my core,
        my strength,
        myself
    rearing to go,
    to live again.

The sorrowful, listless,
    pitiful worm
        inside her pampered cocoon
    is slowly emerging.
A butterfly
    ready to spread her wings
        and fly once more.

★

Two years

I am starting to live again.
Where have I been
   these past two years?

It is as if I am emerging
   from a deep dark pit.
I am amazed
   to find the world still there,
     vibrant in its aliveness.

A heavy blanket of sorrow
   is lifting off my shoulders.
I can move again,
   breathe again.
Enjoy small things,
   feel delight flow
     through my veins
       once more.
Rejoice in my body
   in being healthy,
     in being alive.

✯

2¼ years

My third Christmas and New Year
   without you.
Memories surface
   of those last two times
      when I felt so alone,
      totally bereft,
      abandoned.

Amazed am I
   at the calmness I now feel.
A resigned acceptance
   that you are no longer here
      beside me
   sharing these moments
      with me.

Amazed that those feelings
   of intense pain
      have been transformed with time.

I wanted to cling to that heart-rending grief.
My last tangible link with Job.
Now, even that has gone.

☆

2¼ years

The open wound of grief
   has been covered
      by layers of time.

Upon the raw pain
   the soothing honey
      of 'time gone by'
   has gently nestled its way
      between the jagged nerve ends.

The weeks, months and years
   without you
      form layers of separate existence
         that cover the open wound
            of sorrow.
The moments of joy and pain
   of intimate communication with others
      add layer upon layer
         of soothing balm.

New tissue has been formed.
New life.

Every now and then
   a sensitive spot
      on the scar
         is touched.
The old wound is momentarily alive.

But ever quicker
   the healing layers of time
      soothingly make themselves felt.

2¼ years

Sometimes I feel
   so free,
   so alive,
   so good.
As if a heavy cloud
   has lifted.
A mist that separated me
   from living
     intensely,
     joyously.

When that mist lifts
   to my amazement
   the sun is still shining
     brightly, fiercely.

For so long I had not felt its rays,
   seen its light.
I believed
   it had somehow been extinguished.

Now, it radiates down on me
   warmth,
   zest,
   enthusiasm.
The joy of being alive
   starts to flow once more
     through my being.
Who would have believed it possible?

✪

192

2¼ years

How is it possible
   to feel so good one moment
      and then so terrible the next?

I think: Now I am over it.
Now I can enjoy life again.
Live in the Now.
Forget the past.
Enjoy.

All goes well
   for weeks and weeks.
Then suddenly,
   like a huge beast,
      slowly rising
         from within me
   grief strikes again.

Despair rolls all over me.
I am drenched in sorrow.
I can't shake it off.
I can't imagine
   how gay and carefree I was
      just a week ago.

I go bent
   under the weight
      of a seemingly
      never-ending
         sorrow.

I can't even cry any more.
Just raking dry sobs
   break out
      when the heaviness
         becomes intolerable.

When, oh when
   will this pain
      deep within
   finally leave me?

☆

2¼ years

Sometimes I resent you so
   for having left me.

I feel cold and hard
   towards you.
It hurts less
   than loving you.
It is easier
   to push you away.

But it leaves an emptiness.
A non-feeling.
Depression.

☆

2¼ years

There is a hole in myself,
    that I must fill with *myself*.

Oh, how desperately,
    I would like to fill that hole
        with someone else.

Not to feel this aching emptiness.
This aloneness.
The temptation is so strong
    to use another
        to complete myself.

This I have to learn.
This I must learn;
'Look inside, Kay,
    not outside.'
It is all there
    within me.

I know, I know
    but it is so hard.
The temptation is so strong
    to escape this existential pain,
    to hide within sheltering arms.

You can never really fill yourself
    with another.
You know, you know.
You try to deny.

The potential whole
　　can only be created,
　　can only be discovered,
　　can only be realised
　　　by you
　　　　alone.

2½ years

The worst I could ever have imagined
    happened.
The one I loved the most
    died.
The one I needed the most
    died.
The one I could not live without
    died.

Yet, I survived.

Now, no-one can ever
    wound me so again,
    forsake me so again.

I can still be open
    to pain.
The pain that goes with love.
The pain that tells me
    I live.

However,
    no confrontation,
    no attack,
    no negativity
        can touch or wound
            the *I am*,
            the core within me.

I am free.
Yes, free
   of everyone,
   of everything.

Even though
   I remain
     open,
     loving,
   no-one can claim
     that core within me.
I can live true
   to myself.
Be myself
   completely.

Floating free.
Invincible.

☆

2½ years

All the love
    that used to pour out
        onto you
Is still there.

All that love
    is slowly finding its way,
        not pouring now
        but gently flowing,
    to others.

No longer a mighty waterfall
    but a steadily flowing stream,
        that winds its way
        gently here and there.

It is different, yes,
    but it is still love.
Beautiful in its rewards.
Children, family, friends
    receiving more,
    give more.

I awaken
    to a new dimension
        of living without you.

★

2½ years

He died.
My whole whole world collapsed.
Emptiness.
Nothingness.
A desert.

In this desert
A plant is growing.
   Seeking minute drops
     of moisture everywhere.
   Using all its innate
     resources and creativity
      to survive.
Nourished for the first time
   mainly by itself.
Struggling at first
   but growing ever stronger.
Recognising the peace
   that the desert holds.
     The wide open spaces.
     The freedom.
     The great challenge
      of survival.
Overwhelmed
   by the unexpected beauty
     of the emerging sunrise.

✮

2½ years

I want to
   live again,
   feel again,
   love again.

Ever more impatiently
   these little cries
     are becoming louder and louder.
No longer to be denied.
No longer to be feared.

Life goes on, Kay.
Life is calling you,
   with all its excitement,
     challenges,
     pitfalls,
     and joys.

☆

2½ years

There will never be another
  man
 to my *woman*
But there will be other men.
I accept that now.

You were my *Ur-man*
  to my *Ur-surrendering woman.*

An earthy union
  with deep emotional ties
  with spiritual overtones.

 My Job,
  my man
I thought forever.
Forever is no more.
The woman in me goes on
  and needs man.

I have known *my man*.
I give thanks for that.
I am now at peace,
  open
    to knowing
      other men.

2½ years

Do I dare to love again?
Do I dare to face
    the loss of love again,
        the pain?

What is life
    without love?
Barren, bare.

Kay, dare to live.
Dare to love.
To feel
    the throbbing anticipation,
    the long awaited embrace.

Let go.
Let go
    of your fear.
Allow yourself
    to feel joy once more
        in the closeness
            of another,
        in the love
            of another.
Yes, dare to love
    once more.

Let go.
Let go
    of those nagging thoughts:
'It will never be the same.
It cannot be real.
I am fooling myself.'

Let go
    of thoughts,
    of mind.
Just feel,
    feel.
Be in the *Now*.
Enjoy the *Now*.

✦

2½ years

So good to feel someone
    close, close again.
No, it's not you
    but it's healing.

Human wanting.
Human touch.
Closeness.
Tenderness,
Wildness.

So long barren.
Now slowly starting
    to seep in again.
Becoming alive once more.
Carrying on with the business
    of living.

★

2½ years

No-one will ever
   love me
      like you did,
understand me
      like you did,
cherish me
      like you did.

But I must go on.
I must open up
   to others.

I can no longer deny
   this clamouring inside
      to live,
      to vibrate,
      to feel the touch
         of another.

★

Grindelwald – 2¾ years

Two weeks alone
   in a cottage
      in the Alps.
I come close, close
   to myself
I laugh.
I cry.
I face my weakness.
I find my strength.

Yes, there is only me, now.
Instead of yearning for another's light
   I now live
      in my own light.
If I allow myself
   to feel the rays
      of that light within me
it feels so warm,
   so loving,
   so compassionate,
   so forgiving.

Yes, I am learning
   to vibrate directly
      with the universe
   without having to echo
      life through another.

★

2¾ years – The third message
(Grindelwald – Switzerland)

Under the benign majestic gaze
   of the Eiger and the Jungfrau,
   beside our enchanted stream,
He spoke to me again.

His yearly message.
For nearly an hour
   I feel his words
     swirling around me,
     in me.
So close
   and yet so far away.
So comforting.
So encouraging:

"I love you always.
   Let that strengthen you
     when you are alone
     when you despair,
     when you feel me far away
       remember I am also near.
     Around you,
     around the children,
     around others who need me,
       who think of me."

He urges me not to make my life too complicated.
"Keep it simple.
I smile often
   at your doings,
   at your emotions.

I think: there goes my Kaytje!
I loved you for it, Kay.
But you do go overboard
    and you hurt yourself.
It is so unnecessary.

"I did not desert you, abandon you.
I never have. I never will.
There are forces we don't understand,
    we can't understand.
Don't try to.
Up here, we come closer.
We glimpse more of the Truth.
On Earth, don't think too much.
Let Life flow through you,
    lead you.
It knows where it is going,
    even if you don't.
Enjoy your life.
It is just a game.
The game of life.

"I know you want to know more about me.
I can't convey my life to you.
Not yet.
You don't have the senses to understand
    what it is like to be here.
Know I am 'happy'.
I have found my place now.
I float around in bliss, plentifulness and love.

"Once here, it is all so different.
It is a place of peace
　　of wide open spaces,
　　of unimaginable rest.
You still yearn for earthly delight.
You are not yet ready for the peace.
　　The peace,
　　the nothingness,
　　the allness.
Truly unimaginable on Earth.
Don't even try.
It just is not possible.

"Kaytje, a part of my earthly me
　　lives on in you,
　　in the children,
　　in all who are tied to me.
Dare to draw strength from my presence.
It can no longer hurt you.
Let it flow easily through you."

He ends with:
"Get on with your life, my sweetie.
I love you.
Real love never dies.
It ties forever,
　　through earthly death,
　　through eternity.

"It is so much easier to give of oneself here.
It just flows.
There is no real you or I.
We are all one
　　in Love."

★

Three years

Three years ago
    after you died
I wanted to give up.
I yearned to die.
To be with you always.

In three years' time,
    if life still was so unbearable
        without you
I would finally allow myself
    to slowly fade away
        and die.
I clutched at that straw,
    that promise I made to myself.

Now those years of struggle
    for survival
        lie behind me.

Three years ago, there was no future.
Now, the unknown beckons encouragingly.

Three years ago, I could not get out of bed in the morning.
Now, I feel the gentle pull of the new day ahead.

Three years ago, I could not imagine another man in my life.
Now, all is open.

Three years ago, I felt I had reached the end.
Now, it is as if I am standing
    at the threshold of a new beginning.

No, life is not the same.
It has changed radically.
Yet, I cannot resist the challenge.

One day, I will die anyway.
But, what of the mysteries,
    the lessons,
    the loves
        that still lie ahead?
Yes, I want to face them all,
    no matter how challenging or painful.
I have felt my strength.
I am ready
    to live again.

★

Three years

I still miss you so,
   but
I am making a life
   of my own now.

I cry, I laugh
   about people
      that are not You.
About things
   that have nothing to do with you.

Yes, my life is moving on.
I am living again,
   feeling again,
      without you beside me,
         sheltering me,
         loving me.

I am alone,
   exposed
      but I am surviving.
I am getting stronger
   and stronger
      in my aloneness,
      in my vulnerability.

Less and less do I feel
   I am drowning
      in life's pool.
More and more do I feel
   I am still alive,
      still vibrating.
Standing at the edge
   of that pool
     and challenging life
   while I glide forward
     towards an unknown future.

Three years

Out of the ashes
   of sorrow
I have been reborn.
A very different Kay
   from what I was before.

I was stripped
   of safety, care, the known.
Completely
   alone.

To my amazement
   I rose
     out of nothingness,
     out of seeming death
   into Life once more.

A different world.
Yet, delicately, subtly laden
   with love,
   with freedom.

With open arms
   I now step forward
     to what lies ahead.

Three years

I fell

   deep, deep

      into the abyss.

I came out again

   and found

      a freedom

         unimaginable before.

☆

Three years

Amazing.
A miracle.
Another person is emerging
    from the twosome that was once
        KAY - JOB.

An independent KAY,
    who likes living alone,
    who enjoys the quiet,
    who is not really alone,
    who is loved by some,
    appreciated by others.

A Kay that can radiate
    and shine
        with love,
        enthusiasm
            and life.
Without Job beside her.
Who would have believed
    this possible?

A Kay, that once more
    can intensely enjoy
        moments of living.
The warm feel of the sun.
The movements of her body.
The wind on her skin.
The soft grass under her feet.

She can feel
  not only anguish, sorrow
    and pain
  but peace, love
    and joy again.

Three years

Such a richness
   within me
      of intense feelings,
      of places seen,
      of emotions lived through.

Africa, sun,
   nature, mountains,
      love.

Days gone by:
   Standing on the threshold
      of love.
   Living through its intensity.
   Dying at its sorrow.

Life, life,
   full,
   full.
All smouldering
   within.

I have reached
   a place
      of savouring,
      of rejoicing
   at the wonder
      of really and truly
      having lived through it all.

I can sit back
   and enjoy,
   savour,
   linger.
The present moment
   delicately laden
     with the past.

'I am'
   filled to the brim
     with joys,
     with sorrows,
     with ecstasies
       of days gone by.

A richness within,
   encouraging me
     to go on.

Don't give up, Kay.
Life is full,
   so full.
Don't despair.
Feel what there is,
   laden with what was.

Let yourself flow,
   with this tremendous,
     wondrous
       tide that is life.

✫

Three years

At first I closed myself off
    to the children.
I did not want to burden them
    with my grief.
They had their own lives.
They were also trying to cope.
They could not possibly fill
    that black hole within me.

Now that I am stronger
    I can allow myself
      to feel
        their concern,
        their care.

Trying to keep the delicate balance
    between my need for love
    and their need for independence
I recognise
    and gently bathe
      in the love they shower on me.

Three years

I have learnt to live,
   to enjoy,
     while I lock you
       in a secret place
         deep inside me.

Every now and then,
   when I am alone,
I go within,
   turn the key,
   releasing the pain,
   letting it flow
     easily, comfortingly
       all through me.

I submerge myself
   once more
     in the feel, sorrow
       and nearness of you.

Then I take the key
   and lock you safely
     deep within me
       once more.

Three years

Opening up.
Slowly opening up
   to new loves,
   to new desire,
   to new passion.

Resistance.
Resistance lessens.
Irresistible.
The flow of life.
The eternal interplay
   between man and woman.

Let it come.
Let it flow
   over me,
   around me.
Drowning out
   all those bygone memories.
Sweeping me along
   into the mainstream of life.

Let it come.
This pounding of my blood.
This trembling anticipation.
This throwing myself once more
   into the exciting sea
      of passion.

Standing bravely
 with both arms open
  on the threshold
   of whatever the future
    has in store for me.

Three years

My body is alive,
   vibrating again
     to the touch
       of another.

Life pulsating wildly, deliciously
   through me.

Desire is the opposite of Death.

To feel so alive again,
   young again,
   wanted again.

Delicious, tantalising,
   distracting.
So, so distracting.
Enabling me
   to forget,
   to forget.
Enabling me
   to momentarily
   be in the now
     without sorrow,
     without pain,
     without regrets.

✫

3½ years

I am glad
   I dared to feel
      that intense pain,
      that excruciating loss
         over and over
           again.

By going deep into my pain,
   by allowing myself
      to scream, cry
      and howl out
         all those unbearable feelings
     the burden gradually
       became lighter.
The burden of grief
   that held me bound
      for so long.
Gradually freeing me,
   enabling me to feel
      peaks of joy once more.
Allowing me to experience life
   in a way I had thought not possible
      for me to feel again.

★

3½ years

I thought I could not possibly survive
   and yet I did.
This gives me the strength
   to let go of anxiety
      about the future
  and to allow myself
    the luxury
        of living fully each moment
          as it presents itself to me.

Being intensely in the NOW.
Taking life one step at a time.
Enjoying the peace of this moment.

Feeling strong in the knowledge
   that if I survived
      the loss of that one person closest to me
I can overcome anything.

☆

3½ years

Having seen death
    at such close range
I realise it can strike
    at any moment.
This knowledge urges me
    to make the most of each moment
        while I am still alive.

Do everything I always wanted to do
    Now.
Say everything I want to say
    Now.
Allow myself to enjoy to the full
    Now.
Dare to BE
    that unique person
        that I know I am
    without fear of censure
Now, Now, Now,
    before it is too late.

3½ years

Arms around me.
Closeness.
Intimacy.
Warmth.
Healing.
So, so healing.

The flow of life.
The interaction.

No, it is not you.
I know, I know,
    but it feels so good,
    so right.

It is what I need
    to survive,
    to cope,
    to carry on living.

Feeling the desire,
    the wanting,
    the warmth,
    the vibration,
    the life
        of another
        so close,
        so very close.

The joining.
A yearning,
    momentarily fulfilled,
    giving strength.

The pulse of being
    vibrating strongly
        throughout my body.
Arming me
    to face
        the process of living.

3½ years

Letting myself go
   with a man again.
Letting myself
   be infatuated.

So strange, so strange.
Yet so deliciously
   healing,
   distracting,
   exhilarating.
A natural high.

Not thinking.
Just letting my body,
   my emotions
     take control.
Like a teenager.
A wise old teenager
   indulging herself,
After all that pain.
All that sorrow.
Letting it all go.
For a while.

Just enjoying
   to the full
     this healing
       light-hearted passion.

3½ years

I thought there would be a moment
    when it would be over.
When the sadness, the tears
    would be left behind.
A closed chapter.

I realise now
    that the missing of you
        will always be there.
That in unexpected moments
    the tears,
    the pain
        will rise once more.

As much as I wish
    to start anew
I must accept that you
    and the missing of you
        are still a part of me.

The more I try to convince myself
    that I have left the pain behind
The more I am confronted
    in unexpected moments
        with an 'inexplicable' sadness.

I am strong enough now.
I need no longer
    in vain
        try to deny:
I will always miss him.

✭

3½ years

I have been on a long journey
   through many dark tunnels.

I have been forced to face
   all aspects of Kay.

I have been overwhelmed
   by the love
     I found in myself.

I have also had to humbly accept
   all those dark moods within me:
     the desperation,
     the anger,
     the despair,
     the depression.

Getting to know myself.
Realising to what depths
   I can sink.
Accepting it all
   as part of me.
Forgiving myself
   with love.

Is this the lesson
   I had to learn?

3¾ years – The fourth message
(Grindelwald – Switzerland)

Hiking in the Alps again,
    I near our enchanted stream.
Before I even reach it
    I hear his voice,
        echoing through my being:

"It's over.
Our life together is over.
When will you realise that?
You must go on *alone*.

"It was good for me
    having joined my life to yours
        on earth.
I learnt and felt so much
    through you.
I will be eternally grateful.
I will help you all I can
    but I can do so little from here.
Your guides can help you more.
I can just be a comforting presence.
However, you must first release me
    as I was on earth.
Only then will you be able to open up
    to my presence.
Only then will you perceive me
    as I now am.

"Feel my love more often.
Be strengthened by it.
Feel the love of your guides.
Don't doubt them
    nor their love.
Always have faith in love.
Be open to it from others.
Don't doubt.
As soon as you intuitively feel it
it is there.

"You must learn to be happy
    with what you have
        in the moment.
Happiness comes from within.
It is a state of being.
It is not dependent on anything
    outside of yourself.

"Each day of your life is a gift.
The challenge of living on earth
    is to experience each day to the full.
To feel alive and content
    no matter what befalls us.
Whatever the situation
    pleasant or unpleasant,
It is one's state of mind
    that makes it *feel* good or not.

"It is this state of mind
    that is the real challenge.
It is the essence of this that remains
    after we shed our bodies.

"You are on the right path
   only you get bogged down too often.
You lose sight of your goal.
In this I can help you.
If you open up to my presence
   I can remind you
      when you get lost in the details of living,
   to lift yourself above it all.
   To enjoy the fact that you are alive.

"You have everything in you
   to be able to do this.
      DO IT.
What are you waiting for?
Make the most of each day.
Everything fades away
   except love
      and the way you faced life."

☆

Grindelwald – 3¾ years

As I stroll once more
   along the mountain paths,
      overwhelmed by the mystical beauty
        of the snowy peaks all around me,
I realise how tenaciously I still cling
   to the haunting memories
      of bygone days.

I feel a rising clamouring,
   relentlessly urging me,
   challenging me
To let Job go
   from deep inside me,
      where I surreptitiously
        still hold on to him.

A voice whispers:
   "Have faith,
   realise that although
      he no longer is of flesh and blood,
        nor of this earth,
      he still IS.

   "Dare to let go
      of his *earthly* memory,
      of the longing to hold on to him
        as he was.

"Free yourself
        to open up
                to him as he now IS."

I feel a clutch of fear.
To let go of the *earthly* memory of Job
        would be to finally acknowledge
                that he was physically and emotionally
                        dead to me.

Dare I give up
        that secret, absurd hope
                (as improbable, as illogical
                as it might seem to others)
        of making contact again
                with the protecting, loving
                        Job, as I remembered him?

Inspired by the pristine strength
        of the surrounding Alps,
I feel a rush of energy
        pulsating through me.
In one exhilarating moment
        of wild courage
I LET GO.

Releasing
        the *earthly* Job.
Releasing the past
        once and for all.

Free.
Cleansed.
Open.
I start to perceive Job
    as he now is.
A Being in another realm.
At once the same
    and yet very different
        from what he was on earth.

Stripped of the physical,
    of earthly desire,
    of earthy emotions.
More an essence now
    of wisdom and love.

As I make my way
    down the mountainside
I rejoice:
    I have finally released him.
    Let him go.
The burden of secret longing, pain
    and despair
        has lifted.

I sense his ethereal presence
    gently floating around me
        exuding peace, joy and comfort.

☆

Grindelwald – 3¾ years

Two weeks alone
   in the Alps.
Just the mountains and I.
Feeling happiness
   within me.

Is it possible to be happy
   within oneself
   without the mirror
     of the beloved?

I return to the mysticism
   of childhood,
    where all is one
     within me,
    where the world pulsates
     within my being.
The rushing, rippling stream
   echoes in my ears,
   flows with my blood,
   rousing me to new heights
    of awareness.

To feel all this
   I need no-one
    but myself.
Just open my pores.
Let myself vibrate
   to the music of the universe.

I am beginning
   to find my Self
      after all these years
         of being joined to you.
I realise that
   love,
   passion,
   intensity,
   sorrow
all have their origin
   within me,
      depending on my thoughts,
         my emotions,
         my moods.
I no longer need to see myself
   as being dependent on another.

A shift in perception:
   Happiness, joy, love are not to be found
      outside of myself
   but bubble up from that source within.

☆

Four years

Now it seems like a miracle
    that I lived all those years
      with you.

It is a warm cosy feeling.
No-one can ever take that
    from me.

I will treasure those years
    of love, shelter and support.
They give me the strength, the confidence
    to look to the future
      with optimism,
      with hope.
They form the warm, loving basis
    for the years ahead.

☆

Four years

A word of thanks
  to those 'unseen beings'
    that surround me.

Without their continuous love
  and support
I would not have survived.

I was never completely alone.
In my darkest moments
  they were all there.

Unseen,
  I felt their loving presence
    continuously guiding me,
    encouraging me.
A cloud of 'unconditional love'
  all around me.

With their love and support
  I could not help
    but survive!

See note 1b.

Four years

When you died
   I longed to die with you.
My life seemed over.
Not worth living any more.

But I did not die.
To my amazement
   I continued living,
      feeling,
      being.

I know I too will die
   one day,
   any day.

The challenge is to live
   fully, completely.
Filling the time that remains
   with openness, giving, enjoyment, love.

Daring to face
   and accept with open arms
      all that life has in store for me.

So that when I die
   I can look back
     and say:
"I have truly dared to live."

Four years

Rejoice in being alive.
    Yes, Yes.
Forget you?
    Never.

For all you meant to me.
For all we shared.
For the love,
    the comfort,
    the strength,
    the support
You gave
    and still give.

No, I will never forget you.

Notes

1. The death.

1a. Silver cord:
Some people believe that our 'etheric body' or soul is attached to our earthly body by a 'silver' cord. (Psychics say they can perceive this cord.) When we die this cord is broken and the soul is freed from the body. The cutting of Job's silver cord can also be seen as symbolically letting him go. Job probably felt my longing that he remain alive. When I called on my guides to help cut his silver cord, he may intuitively have felt that I was willing to let him go, thus enabling him to die.

1b. My guides:
Since I was a child, I have every now and then felt the presence of 'unseen beings'. Whether they are real or not, I cannot know for sure. I do know that in moments of extreme stress or great happiness I feel supported or guided by them.

1c. Reliving the death:
I relived Job's death many times. At first ('The Death': p. 17), it was the memory of his bliss and his sense of freedom that lingered within me.

Later ('Rebirthing – 13 months': p. 90), came the memories of the agony of desperately wanting him to live, yet actually helping him to die.

It was only after two years that, on reliving his death once again (p. 184), I could *start* to face the fact that he had actually died that night and that the body lying next to me was a corpse.

2. The coffin. The memorial service. The burial.:
Job's coffin rested in our bedroom (except during the memorial service) till the day of his burial. The memorial

247

service took place the evening before the day that he was buried.

3a. Grindelwald:

For years, Job and I used to go to Switzerland each summer. We stayed alone, together in a chalet high in the mountains above the village of Grindelwald. After his death, I continued coming alone, each July, to the same chalet in Grindelwald.

3b. The messages:

I leave it to the reader to decide whether these messages really came from the deceased Job or not. To me, it seemed as if I were really communicating with him and the messages proved to be of invaluable emotional support to me.

4. Rebirthing:

A form of quick superficial breathing, sometimes accompanied by music, that, among other things, can help reduce resistance to suppressed emotions, enabling them to be expressed.

5. Love song AD 1200:

One of my favourite poems – a German ballad from the Middle Ages – suddenly took on a new meaning for me. I translated it, as it described what I felt at that moment.

6. Dancing to African music:

This 'trance-dancing' is done in a group, with one's eyes closed, accompanied by African drummers.

Translations

The Death:

"*ijsklontjes*" :

"ice cubes"
(It was difficult for him to drink water.)

"*Nu wil ik stoppen.... Het komt....*" :

"Now I want to stop.
It is over
    with Job.
Finished, full stop, the end.
Now I want to go into the Self,
As quickly as possible Home.
It is fantastic.
This is it...
Not quite yet.
It is coming...."

"*Je gaat Job!*" :

"You are going, Job!"

"*Het is zo mooi ... vrij*" :

"It is so beautiful, Kay.
Indescribable.
Fantastic, wonderful.
Wide (open spaces), free.
Free, at last."

10 days later:

"*Job, nu is het genoeg.*":

"Job, it is enough, now."

5 months later:

"*En dit is mijn Kay.*":

"And this is my Kay."

20 months:

"*Goed zo Kaytje. Ga zo door.*":

"Well done, Kaytje. Keep it up."
(Kaytje = little Kay = pet name)

1¾ years – The second message:

"*Dag lief Kaytje.*":

"Goodbye sweet Kaytje."

"*Tot de volgende keer langs deze beek?*":

"Till the next time, beside this stream?"